DISCARDED

Full Count

Top 10 Lists of Everything in BASEBALL

Managing Editor, Sports Illustrated Kids **Bob Der**

Creative Director **Beth Bugler**

Project Editor **Andrea Woo**

Director of Photography **Marguerite Schropp Lucarelli**

Photo Editors **Porter Binks, Annmarie Avila**

Writers **Gary Gramling, Matthew Harrigan,
Christina M. Tapper, Paul Ulane, Eli Bernstein**

Editors **Justin Tejada, Sachin Shenolikar**

Copy Editor **Megan Collins**

Designer **Kirsten Sorton**

Imaging **Geoffrey Michaud, Dan Larkin, Robert Thompson**

TIME HOME ENTERTAINMENT
Publisher: Richard Fraiman
Vice President, Business Development & Strategy: Steven Sandonato
Executive Director, Marketing Services: Carol Pittard
Executive Director, Retail & Special Sales: Tom Mifsud
Executive Publishing Director: Joy Butts
Director, Bookazine Development & Marketing: Laura Adam
Finance Director: Glenn Buonocore
Associate Publishing Director: Megan Pearlman
Assistant General Counsel: Helen Wan
Assistant Director, Special Sales: Ilene Schreider
Senior Book Production Manager: Susan Chodakiewicz
Design & Prepress Manager: Anne-Michelle Gallero
Brand Manager: Allison Parker
Associate Prepress Manager: Alex Voznesenskiy
Assistant Brand Manager: Stephanie Braga

Editorial Director: Stephen Koepp

SPECIAL THANKS TO: Christine Austin, Katherine Barnet, Jeremy Biloon, Jim Childs,
Rose Cirrincione, Lauren Hall Clark, Jacqueline Fitzgerald, Christine Font,
Jenna Goldberg, Hillary Hirsch, Suzanne Janso, Amy Mangus, Robert Marasco,
Kimberly Marshall, Amy Migliaccio, Nina Mistry, Dave Rozzelle, Adriana Tierno, Vanessa Wu

ISBN 10: 1-61893-006-0
ISBN 13: 978-1-61893-006-4
Library of Congress Number: 2012938319
Sports Illustrated Kids is a trademark of Time Inc.
We welcome your comments and suggestions about Sports Illustrated Kids Books.
Please write to us at:
    Sports Illustrated Kids Books
    Attention: Book Editors
    P.O. Box 11016
    Des Moines, IA 50336-1016
If you would like to order any of our hardcover Collector's Edition books, please call
us at 1-800-327-6388 (Monday through Friday, 7:00 a.m. – 8:00 p.m. Central Time,
or Saturday, 7:00 a.m. – 6:00 p.m. Central Time).

Lovable Lou Seal of the San Francisco Giants is one of the 10 greatest mascots of all time.

The Top 10 Lists

New York Yankees shortstop Derek Jeter is among our Top 10 future Hall of Famers.

Top 10 Leadoff

1

Rickey Henderson
Leftfielder
MLB Career: 1979–2003

Whether with the longball or a base on balls, Henderson knew how to get on base and put runs on the scoreboard. The Hall of Famer's combination of speed and power helped him set major league career records for stolen bases (1,406), runs scored (2,295), and leadoff home runs (293). Henderson paced two World Series–champion lineups: the 1989 Oakland A's and the 1993 Toronto Blue Jays.

2 **Tim Raines**
Leftfielder
MLB Career: 1979–2002

He was nicknamed Rock because of his stocky stature, but Raines could fly. The seven-time All-Star not only got on base (.385 career on-base percentage), he also was dangerous on the base paths, leading the NL in stolen bases four times while playing for the Montreal Expos.

3 **Lou Brock**
Leftfielder
MLB Career: 1961–79

Brock is known as a great table setter because of his speed: He won eight stolen-base titles in his 19-year career. The six-time All-Star also had a career .293 batting average with 3,023 hits and 938 stolen bases. He helped lead the St. Louis Cardinals to two World Series championships.

4 **Pete Rose**
Outfielder/Infielder
MLB Career: 1963–86

Baseball's all-time hits leader was the spark plug of the Reds' World Series–winning teams in the 1970s. Rose was a steady presence in the lineup, rarely taking a day off (he holds the major league mark for games played with 3,562). He won three NL batting titles and led the league in runs four times.

5 **Billy Hamilton**
Outfielder
MLB Career: 1888–1901

Hamilton, who played mostly in the 1800s, has been in the record books for a long time. He has the fourth-highest on-base percentage (.455) in major league history, scored a single-season-record 198 runs in 1894, and is one of three players to finish his career with more runs scored than games played.

Hitters

6 **Ichiro Suzuki**
Rightfielder
MLB Career: 2001–present

The Mariners great is one of the best hitters to ever play the game. Ichiro has the all-time highest batting average among leadoff men (.326 through 2011). The two-time AL batting champ has led the league in hits seven times.

7 **Johnny Damon**
Outfielder
MLB Career: 1995–present

Damon, who jump-started the Red Sox's run to the World Series in 2004, is a leadoff man with power, patience, and speed. In 2000, he led the AL in runs and steals. Through 2011, Damon had 163 leadoff home runs, fifth most all-time.

8 **Craig Biggio**
Second Baseman
MLB Career: 1988–2007

In 20 years in the majors, all with the Houston Astros, Biggio found many ways to get on base. The second baseman led the league in hit by pitches five times and finished with a career on-base percentage of .363.

9 **Jose Reyes**
Shortstop
MLB Career: 2003–present

With a big bat and blazing speed, Reyes is one of the best leadoff hitters in today's game. The four-time All-Star has led the NL in triples four times and stolen bases three times. He also won a batting crown with the Mets in 2011.

10 **Paul Molitor**
Infielder/DH
MLB Career: 1978–98

Molitor lived up to his nickname, the Ignitor. Hitting at the top of the Brewers' lineup for 15 seasons, Molitor led the AL in runs three times and helped Milwaukee win the pennant in 1982. He ranks fourth all-time in career leadoff doubles (338).

UNBREAKABLE RECORDS

1 Cal Ripken Jr.'s 2,632 consecutive games

When you take a closer look at the numbers, Ripken's consecutive-games streak is simply staggering. He played every game from May 30, 1982, through September 19, 1998, a span of 17 seasons. Lou Gehrig's 2,130 consecutive-games streak was supposed to be untouchable, and Ripken not only broke it, he went on to play every contest for three more seasons. No one besides Gehrig has even reached the halfway point of Ripken's streak. According to MLB.com, a young Derek Jeter once asked Ripken what his secret was. Ripken's answer was simple: "I just love to play, and it kind of happened."

Nolan Ryan's 5,714 career strikeouts

Ryan is arguably the most dominant pitcher of all time. No other player has even reached the 5,000-strikeout plateau. The Ryan Express also holds the single-season strikeout record for the modern era (383 in 1973). The fact that he played in parts of 27 seasons definitely helped him collect such a huge total, but Ryan's ability can't be questioned. He struck out 301 batters in 1989, when he was 42 years old. There hasn't been a 300-strikeout season since 2002.

Joe DiMaggio's 56-game hit streak (1941)

Two months of hot hitting doesn't seem that tough, but the pursuit of Joltin' Joe's record puts more pressure on a player than any other. One bad day, or a couple of nice plays by fielders, and you're back to zero. Pete Rose came the closest to DiMaggio's mark, but the Hit King's streak was snapped at 44 in 1978. More recently, Philadelphia Phillies shortstop Jimmy Rollins had a 38-game streak that started at the end of the 2005 season and lasted into the beginning of '06. No one has topped 38 games since. It's worth noting that two minor leaguers have had longer streaks. In 1919, Joe Wilhoit of the Wichita Jobbers hit safely in 69 straight games. And in 1933, a San Francisco Seals outfielder had hits in 61 consecutive games — his name was Joe DiMaggio.

Hack Wilson's 191 RBIs (1930)

How impressive was Wilson's 1930 season? The Chicago Cubs Hall of Famer was still picking up RBIs 69 years after the season ended. He was originally credited with 190 RBIs, but in 1999 a scoring error was discovered in a 1930 box score. Wilson got the 191st RBI added to his record 51 years after he died. Since the 1930s, no one has come closer to Wilson's mark than Manny Ramirez's 165 RBIs in 1999.

Cy Young's 511 career wins

It's no wonder the top pitching award is named after Young. Only one other pitcher, Walter Johnson, has even topped 400 wins (417). Young's record will never be bested because of the way the game has changed. In 1892, Young threw 453 innings over 53 games. That's two seasons' worth of innings for a starting pitcher in today's game. With five-man rotations and specialized bullpens, current starting pitchers are throwing fewer innings than ever. And the earlier that pitchers get pulled, the fewer decisions (wins and losses) they have.

Pete Rose's 4,256 career hits

The weird thing about Rose's all-time hits record is that he was never a consistently great hitter. In 24 seasons he won only three batting titles, and he never hit higher than .348 in a season. His career .303 batting average is tied for 174th best of all time, behind such current players as the Texas Rangers'

Michael Young and the Detroit Tigers' Victor Martinez. But Rose was a very good hitter for a very long time, and he rarely missed time because of injuries. His 3,562 career games are much more than any other player in baseball history.

Rickey Henderson's 130 stolen bases (1982)

Henderson's modern-day steals record won't be topped, but he didn't stand out only for being very, very fast. Unlike a lot of today's speedsters, he was an on-base machine throughout his career. He hit only .267 in 1982, but he drew 116 walks, giving him a .398 on-base percentage. The era he played in also helped boost his record. Managers were far more aggressive on the base paths in the 1980s. There have been eight 100-stolen-base seasons in baseball's modern era, and six took place in that decade.

Ty Cobb's .366 career batting average

Depending on whom you ask, Cobb's career average might actually have been .367 (baseball didn't keep great track of stats back then). But regardless of the exact number, no one is coming close to it. Cobb never hit less than .316 in a full season, and his .420 average in 1911 is the fourth highest of the modern era. Heading into 2012, Albert Pujols was the active leader in career batting average, at .328. If he were to play another 10 seasons, he'd have to hit somewhere in the neighborhood of .404 over the rest of his career to catch Cobb.

Orel Hershiser's 59 consecutive scoreless innings (1988)

In 1968, Don Drysdale threw 58 consecutive scoreless innings to break Walter Johnson's record of 55⅔. That year, Bob Gibson threw 47 straight shutout innings, and Luis Tiant's scoreless streak reached 41. Pitchers were so dominant in '68 that baseball lowered the mound from 15 inches to 10 inches to take some of the advantage away from hurlers. In large part because of that change, no one came close to Drysdale's record until Hershiser went on his incredible run 20 years later. Hershiser's streak wasn't just impressive, it propelled the Dodgers to a World Series win that season.

Hank Aaron's 25 All-Star Game appearances

Hammerin' Hank didn't make the All-Star Game as a rookie in 1954. And he didn't make it in his final season, in 1976. But he made it every year in between, playing in his first All-Star Game at age 21 and his last one at age 41. Playing in 21 years of All-Star Games is a record, and Aaron's game total is inflated by the fact that for four seasons (1959–62) there were two All-Star Games per season. In 2011, 21-year-old Chicago Cubs shortstop Starlin Castro made the NL All-Star team. To catch Aaron, he'll have to make the midsummer classic every year until he's 45.

TOP 10 LITTLE

6' 5"
6' 0"
5' 6"
5' 0"
4' 6"
4' 0"
3' 6"
3' 0"

1 Eddie Gaedel
Pinch Hitter
HT: 3' 7" WT: 65 lbs
In 1951, Gaedel was hired by the St. Louis Browns to pull off a zany stunt. After jumping out of a cake between games of a doubleheader, Gaedel strolled to the plate in the first inning. He walked on four straight pitches before being removed for a pinch runner, but his place in baseball lore was forever secured.

2 Wee Willie Keeler
Rightfielder
HT: 5' 4" WT: 140 lbs
This Hall of Famer had a simple recipe for success: "Hit 'em where they ain't." The approach worked well for Keeler. Toting a hefty 46-ounce bat, one of the heaviest in baseball, he finished his career with a .345 batting average.

3 Freddie Patek
Shortstop
HT: 5' 5" WT: 148 lbs
When you get a nickname like the Flea, chances are you're a little guy. Patek, who barely reached 5'5", hustled his way onto three American League All-Star teams and led the league in triples in 1971 and in steals in '77.

4 Phil Rizzuto
Shortstop
HT: 5' 6" WT: 150 lbs
Rizzuto never let size get in the way of winning over a 13-season career that was interrupted for three years during World War II. Nicknamed Scooter, he anchored the Yankees' middle infield for seven World Series–winning teams.

5 David Eckstein
Shortstop
HT: 5' 6" WT: 170 lbs
Eckstein had a huge impact on two World Series–winning teams. In 2002, he led the Angels in runs and was second in hits. At the 2006 World Series, Eckstein tied for the team lead in hits and RBIs and took home the World Series MVP trophy with the Cardinals.

GUYS

6' 5"

6' 0"

5' 6"

5' 0"

4' 6"

3' 6"

3' 0"

6 **Joe Morgan**
Second Baseman
HT: 5' 7" **WT:** 160 lbs
This two-time NL MVP was the conductor of Cincinnati's famed Big Red Machine teams of the mid-1970s. Known for his speed — he had 40 or more steals nine times in his career — he also packed some punch (268 career home runs).

7 **Yogi Berra**
Catcher
HT: 5' 7" **WT:** 185 lbs
Berra isn't just one of the most quotable ballplayers ever; he's also one of the best catchers of all time. The perennial Yankees All-Star won three American League MVPs, 14 pennants, and 10 World Series in a 19-year career.

8 **Kirby Puckett**
Centerfielder
HT: 5' 8" **WT:** 178 lbs
The outfielder was known for his happy-go-lucky style on the field, but his career achievements were no joke. Puckett won six Gold Gloves and made 10 straight All-Star teams. He led the Twins to World Series wins in 1987 and '91.

9 **Dustin Pedroia**
Second Baseman
HT: 5' 9" **WT:** 180 lbs
Pedroia burst onto the scene by winning the Rookie of the Year award in 2007 as a second baseman for the Red Sox. In 2008, the man they call the Laser Show sprayed enough line drives to take home the American League MVP award.

10 **Tim Lincecum**
Pitcher
HT: 5' 10" **WT:** 165 lbs
The pitcher known simply as the Freak got his nickname for his amazing ability to generate 95-mile-per-hour fastballs from such a small frame. It's a skill that has helped him win two National League Cy Young Awards and a World Series title in his first five seasons in the majors.

1

Andruw Jones

Centerfielder, MLB Career: 1996–present

Neither an outfield wall nor a face-plant into turf could stop Jones from making an amazing catch. Breaking into the big leagues as a 19-year-old, he immediately established himself as a defensive great. Jones won 10 consecutive Gold Gloves from 1998 to 2007 while playing centerfield for the Atlanta Braves. He covered a huge amount of ground, and his diving catches regularly made highlight reels. "You're going to get hurt sometimes when you dive," Jones told ESPN.com in 2004. "But you don't think about that. You're trying to make a play. That's what you get paid for; that's what you've dreamed about."

Top 10 Hit R

PPLY

COMPANY

1923

obbers

2 Tris Speaker
Centerfielder, MLB Career: 1907–28

Speaker may have been overshadowed by his contemporary Ty Cobb, who was a better all-around player, but few in baseball history can match Speaker's defense in centerfield. Revolutionizing the position, Speaker was the first outfielder to play shallow to ensure that hits would not fall in front of him. He led the American League in putouts seven

times in an 11-year span (1909 to '19, while with the Red Sox and Indians). With uncanny instincts and great speed, Speaker finished his career with 6,788 putouts, second all-time, during an era in which few balls were hit to the outfield.

3 Richie Ashburn
Centerfielder, MLB Career: 1948–62

Ashburn played during the same era as Willie Mays, Mickey Mantle, and Duke Snider, so he didn't get much attention outside of Philadelphia, where he spent 12 years as an outfielder for the Phillies. Ashburn was a lightning-quick leadoff hitter, but it was in the field where he really shined. He led the National League in outfield putouts nine times in his 15-year career. There have been only eight 500-putout seasons in MLB history, and Ashburn had four of them.

6 Jim Edmonds
Centerfielder
MLB Career: 1993–2010

Edmonds, who spent most of his career manning centerfield for the Angels and Cardinals, was a regular on the highlight shows in the 1990s and 2000s. For one particular catch in Kansas City in 1997, he ran backward and laid out to make a diving catch on the warning track. It was one of the greatest plays ever made.

7 Max Carey
Outfielder, MLB Career: 1910–29

Carey was known for his blazing speed, but it was his instincts that helped make him one of the all-time defensive greats. The longtime Pirate led the National League in putouts nine times in his 20-year career. He earned the nickname

Scoops for his ability to track down balls quickly and throw out base runners. While a lot of players slow down once they reach their 30s, three of Carey's finest defensive seasons were 1921 to '23, after he turned 31 years old.

4 Curt Flood
Centerfielder, MLB Career: 1956–71

Flood is most famous for his work off the field: The centerfielder fought for players' rights at a time when teams had complete control over their careers, and he paved the way for free agency. But on the field, he was one of the greatest defensive players ever. A premier speedster of the 1960s, he ran down everything in St. Louis. He won seven consecutive Gold Gloves with the Cardinals from 1963 to '69, and led the National League in outfield putouts four times in his career.

5 Willie Mays, *Centerfielder*
MLB Career: 1951–52, '54–73

Typically, the best defensive outfielders are slender speedsters. Mays, on the other hand, was a muscular 5'10", 170 pounds — a power hitter who was built like a tank. Despite that, he had excellent speed and amazing instincts, covering a ton of ground in New York's spacious Polo Grounds (where the centerfield wall was 483 feet from home plate). Mays won 11 Gold Glove awards, and his 7,095 career outfield putouts are the most in baseball history.

8 Dom DiMaggio
Centerfielder, MLB Career: 1940–42, '46–53

The DiMaggio brothers — Joe, Dom, and Vince — were all terrific players. Joe became a legend playing for the New York Yankees, but it was Dom who stood out when it came to amazing glove work in centerfield. Even Joe agreed, calling his younger brother "the best defensive outfielder I've ever seen." Patrolling Fenway Park's spacious centerfield for the Boston Red Sox in the 1940s and early '50s, Dom DiMaggio led the American League in putouts twice.

9 Paul Blair
Centerfielder, MLB Career: 1964–80

The Baltimore Orioles' pitchers had some outstanding statistical seasons during the 1960s and '70s. As great as their arms were, a big reason the O's got so many outs was that Blair was manning centerfield, turning would-be base hits into outs. A fleet-footed fielder who covered more ground than anyone in the American League during that era, Blair won eight Gold Glove awards in his career. He led the AL in outfield putouts twice in his first five full seasons.

10 Ty Cobb
Centerfielder, MLB Career: 1905–28

Cobb is known for his many accomplishments at the plate, but he was also an all-time great in the field. Cobb was a speedy and extremely aggressive centerfielder for the Detroit Tigers. He consistently got to balls in the outfield that others couldn't have reached. He committed a whopping 271 errors in his career, but all the tough plays he made compensated for the miscues. His 6,361 putouts are the third most of all time by an outfielder.

TOP 10 Nicknames

1 The Babe, The Bambino, The Sultan of Swat

George Herman Ruth, *Outfielder*

Ruth was such a big star that one nickname was not enough. He is commonly known by his original nickname, Babe, given to Ruth as a 19-year-old rookie. From there, the many Yankees fans of Italian descent translated Babe to Bambino. Then, as he became one of the greatest sluggers in baseball — he finished his career with 714 home runs — the Sultan of Swat was added as a nod to Ruth's heroics at the plate.

2 The Wizard of Oz

Ozzie Smith
Shortstop

A 13-time Gold Glove winner, Smith earned his nickname by making some of the most magical plays ever seen at shortstop. The Hall of Famer's athleticism was on display before games, when he drew cheers by performing a cartwheel and a backflip as he ran onto the field.

3 The Say Hey Kid

Willie Mays
Centerfielder

One of the most famous nicknames in baseball has murky origins. According to sportswriter Barney Kremenko, Mays would shout, "Say who, say what, say where, say hey," during his rookie season. Others claim that in the minor leagues Mays didn't know his teammates' names, so he would call out, "Hey" if he needed them.

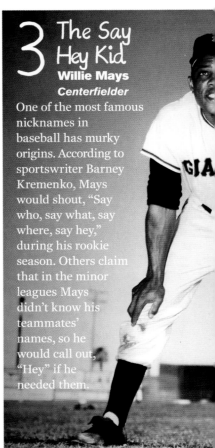

7 Big Papi

David Ortiz
Designated Hitter

When Ortiz arrived in Boston in 2003, he didn't know any of his new teammates by name, so he just called everyone Papi. Players on the Sox returned the favor, but since the slugger was a hulking 6' 4" and 230 pounds, it was natural that he would become *Big* Papi.

4 The Kid
Ken Griffey Jr., *Centerfielder*

One of the best all-around centerfielders to play the game, Griffey made his debut at 19 and kept his youthful attitude throughout his 22-year career. Known for wearing his hat backward during batting practice, Griffey had a sweet lefthanded swing and a flair for dramatic outfield catches.

5 Wild Thing
Mitch Williams, *Pitcher*

Let's just say that Williams wasn't a master of pitch control. With 544 career walks, he made almost every save situation an adventure. Despite Williams's three seasons with at least 30 saves, his most famous moment was a blown save against the Blue Jays in the final game of the 1993 World Series.

6 Shoeless Joe
Joe Jackson, *Outfielder*

After getting blisters from a new pair of cleats in the first game of a 1908 semi-pro doubleheader, Jackson decided to play the second game without shoes. When he hit a triple in the seventh inning, Jackson was called a "shoeless son of a gun" by a fan, and the nickname stuck.

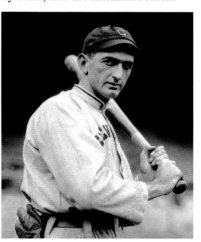

8 The Spaceman
Bill Lee, *Pitcher*

Lee won 119 games over a 14-year career, but he earned his nickname with far-out quotes like, "Do you realize that even as we sit here, we are hurtling through space at a tremendous rate of speed? Think about it. Our world is just a hanging curveball."

10 Kung Fu Panda
Pablo Sandoval
Third Baseman

Despite his hefty frame, the Giants' rotund third baseman is deceptively athletic. San Francisco pitcher Barry Zito dubbed him Kung Fu Panda (for the cartoon character) after Sandoval jumped over a catcher to score a run in a 2008 game.

9 The Bird
Mark Fidrych
Pitcher

Fidrych got his nickname from a minor league coach who thought he looked like Big Bird. The lanky 6'3" 175-pounder with floppy blond hair bursting out from under his cap even appeared on the cover of SPORTS ILLUSTRATED with the *Sesame Street* character. As a rookie in 1976, Fidrych won 19 games.

TOP 10
HARDEST THROWERS

1 Nolan Ryan
MLB Career: 1966–93

In 1974, Ryan's fastball was clocked at 100.9 miles per hour, then a record. But the technology used to clock pitches has improved greatly over the past decade. Some now have estimated that Ryan's heater actually traveled at 108.1 miles per hour. If you told that to any of the record 5,714 batters Ryan struck out during his 27-year career, they'd have no trouble believing it.

2 Satchel Paige
Negro Leagues Career: 1926–48, MLB Career: 1948–53, '65
Paige dominated in the Negro Leagues for the first part of his career and — even though he didn't pitch in the majors until age 42 — overpowered big-league hitters as well. Paige basically threw only fastballs, giving them nicknames like Long Tommy, Bat Dodger, Be Ball, and Midnight Rider. Even though hitters knew what was coming, Paige's pitches came in so fast that they still couldn't hit them.

3 Aroldis Chapman
MLB Career: 2010–present
The young lefthander from Cuba is a fearsome fireballer. He owns the official mark for the fastest pitch ever recorded by Pitch f/x, the best technology for tracking a pitcher's velocity. The 6'4" Chapman buzzed a fastball that was recorded at 105.1 miles per hour, as a rookie with the Cincinnati Reds in September 2010.

4 Walter Johnson
MLB Career: 1907–27
There's no way of knowing exactly how hard Johnson threw his fastball. But in 1917, a lab brought in three flamethrowers — Johnson, Christy Mathewson, and Smoky Joe Wood — and measured how far their pitches traveled in one second. The Washington Senators ace beat out the field with a ball that went 134 feet.

5 Bob Feller
MLB Career: 1936–41, '45–56
In 1940 Feller was part of a grand experiment to see how fast he could throw a fastball. A motorcycle raced past Feller at 86 miles per hour, getting a 10-foot head start before Feller fired a perfect strike. The baseball hit its target a split second before the motorcycle did. The pitch was estimated at 104 miles per hour.

6 Joe Williams
Negro Leagues Career: 1905–32
With a nearly untouchable fastball, Williams regularly racked up 20 strikeouts in games. In an exhibition game in 1912, he shut out the NL-champion New York Giants. At age 44, Williams punched out 27 batters in a 12-inning Negro Leagues game.

7 Joel Zumaya
MLB Career: 2006–present
Before injuries struck, Zumaya was quite a fireballer. In 2009 and '10, his fastball averaged more than 99 miles per hour. As a rookie with the Detroit Tigers in '06, Zumaya struck out 97 in 83⅓ innings, holding opponents to a .187 batting average.

8 J.R. Richard
MLB Career: 1971–80
The 6'8" Richard was a phenom in high school as a pitcher and power hitter. After learning to harness his fastball, he struck out more than 300 batters in 1978 and '79 with the Astros. He was having a career year in 1980, before he suffered a stroke that ended his career at age 30.

9 Herb Score
MLB Career: 1955–62
Armed with a blazing fastball, the lefty struck out a then-rookie-record 245 hitters in 1955 and a league-leading 263 in '56. Score also won 20 games that season. Unfortunately, he was hit in the face by a line drive in 1957 and was never the same pitcher after the incident.

10 Smoky Joe Wood
MLB Career: 1908–20
"No man alive can throw any harder than Smoky Joe Wood," Walter Johnson once said. The righthander had a career 2.03 ERA and won three World Series over 11 big-league seasons with the Red Sox and Indians.

Top 10
RIVALR

1 New York Yankees– Boston Red Sox

This is the rivalry against which all others are measured, not only in baseball, but in all sports. The Red Sox were the winners of the first World Series and had five championships by 1918. Then fortunes turned in favor of the Yankees. Boston sent its star pitcher, Babe Ruth, to New York in 1919, and the Red Sox's title drought — known as the Curse of the Bambino — officially began. Over the next 85 years, the Yankees won 26 championships and the Red Sox won none. In 2004, the Red Sox looked as if they were going to fall victim to the curse once again, trailing three games to none in the ALCS against who else but the Yankees. Refusing to give up, Boston made an improbable comeback to win the series in seven games and rode that momentum to a World Series title. With both teams fighting for the top spot in the AL East year after year, the rivalry remains as heated as ever.

2 Brooklyn/Los Angeles Dodgers—New York/San Francisco Giants

This rivalry dates back to the mid-1900s in New York, when the Dodgers played at Ebbets Field in Brooklyn and the Giants at the Polo Grounds in upper Manhattan. One of the rivalry's most famous moments came in 1951, when Giants third baseman Bobby Thomson hit the Shot Heard 'Round the World — a walk-off home run that clinched the NL pennant against the Dodgers. After the 1957 season, both teams moved to California, where the rivalry continues. Through 2011, each franchise has won 21 NL pennants and six World Series titles.

3 **New York Yankees—Los Angeles Dodgers**
The Yankees and the Dodgers have faced off 11 times in the World Series (eight of which were won by the Bronx Bombers). The matchup — which began when the Dodgers played in Brooklyn — has led to some of baseball's most magical Fall Classic moments. Among them: Dodgers legend Jackie Robinson stealing home in 1955, Yankees pitcher Don Larsen's perfect game in 1956, Dodgers ace Sandy Koufax's two complete-game wins in 1963, and Yankees slugger Reggie Jackson earning the name Mr. October with his five home runs in 1977.

4 **Chicago White Sox—Chicago Cubs**
Before interleague play was introduced in 1997, these teams had met only once, in the 1906 World Series, which the White Sox won. But this rivalry has always been fierce, thanks to the loyal Chicago fans. In Chicago, there are North Siders (Cubs supporters) and South Siders (White Sox fans), and each openly roots against the crosstown team, no matter whom they are playing. Through 2011, the White Sox have the edge in the head-to-head series, 49–41, as well as in the number of World Series won (3–2).

7 **Chicago Cubs—St. Louis Cardinals**
Called the I-55 Series after the road that connects St. Louis and Chicago, the rivalry between the Cubs and the Cardinals dates back to 1892. The cities are less than 300 miles apart, and linking them even more closely is the fact that several baseball legends have played for both teams. Slugger Rogers Hornsby holds the single-season hits record for both the Cubs and the Cardinals. Even longtime Cubs announcer Harry Caray began his career in St. Louis. Chicago holds the series lead (1,166–1,104 through 2011), but St. Louis has nine more World Series titles (11).

8 **Tampa Bay Rays—Boston Red Sox**
The Rays–Red Sox rivalry peaked on the last night of the 2011 regular season, even though the two teams weren't even playing each other. That night, the Rays came back from a seven-run deficit to defeat the Yankees in extra innings just minutes after the Red Sox blew a ninth-inning lead and lost to the Orioles. The events completed an epic collapse by the Sox, who went 7–20 in September to lose the wild card to the Rays. Tampa won the only playoff series in which the two teams have squared off, but Boston leads the series 144–101 overall.

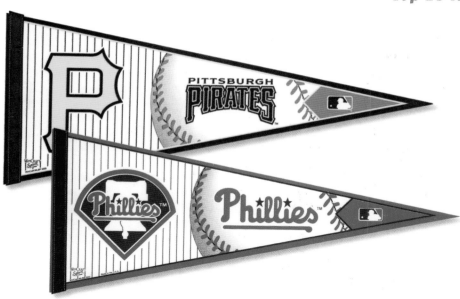

5 Pittsburgh Pirates—Philadelphia Phillies

The Pirates and the Phillies once had the most intense rivalry in the National League. Between 1970 and '80, either Pittsburgh or Philadelphia won 10 of 11 NL East titles. They also combined for three World Series championships over that span. In 126 games from 1974 to '80, the intrastate rivals split the series 63–63. The matchup lost some intensity when the Pirates moved to the NL Central in 1994. Despite the Pirates' recent struggles and the Phillies' recent success, the Pirates still led the series 1,098–918 through the 2011 season.

6 New York Mets—Philadelphia Phillies

When the Mets traded centerfielder Lenny Dykstra and pitcher Roger McDowell to the Phillies in June 1989, it set the stage for years of tension between New York and Philadelphia. During the 1989 and '90 seasons, two bench-clearing brawls broke out between them, one as a result of McDowell trash-talking his old teammates. When the 1994 National League realignment moved the Pirates to the Central, the Mets became the Phillies' top NL East foes. Eighteen years later, Mets-Phillies remains one of the nastiest rivalries in the NL.

9 Atlanta Braves—New York Mets

Though the Miracle Mets swept the Braves in the 1969 NLCS, the rivalry between the two teams didn't really start until the Braves moved to the NL East in 1994. The bad blood was at its height in the late '90s and early 2000s, when the Braves dominated the division and the Mets were the scrappy underdogs. When the two teams faced off in the 1999 NLCS, Atlanta needed six games to win despite going up 3–0 to start the series. In 2000, the Mets finished ahead of the Braves to earn a spot in the playoffs.

10 Los Angeles Angels—Texas Rangers

The Angels and Rangers are the newest rivalry in the majors. The Angels controlled the AL West in the 2000s, making the playoffs six times and winning the World Series in 2002. But the Rangers have established themselves as the new AL West power with back-to-back World Series appearances, in 2010 and '11. Before the 2012 season, the Angels upped the stakes, signing the best player in baseball, Albert Pujols, to refuel their rivalry with Texas.

Top 10 Single-Game Performances

1 Harvey Haddix: 12 perfect innings pitched (May 26, 1959)

It was the greatest pitching performance of all time — even though it resulted in a loss. With his Pittsburgh Pirates unable to put a run on the board, Haddix pitched a perfect game into extra innings. He retired 36 batters in a row until finally, in the bottom of the 13th, the Milwaukee Braves ended the perfect game when their batter reached base on an error. Later in the inning, Haddix lost his no-hitter, his shutout, and the game when the Braves' Joe Adcock blasted a pitch into the seats.

2 Carlos Delgado: Four home runs in four plate appearances (September 25, 2003)

Talk about discovering your home run swing. While 15 players have hit four home runs in a game, the Blue Jays' Delgado is the only slugger to do it each time he came to the plate.

3 Kerry Wood: 20 strikeouts against 29 batters (May 6, 1998)

In Wood's fifth career start, the Chicago Cubs rookie righthander struck out 20 Houston Astros batters, tying the major league record set by Roger Clemens for a nine-inning game. Wood finished with a one-hit shutout and allowed only two base runners.

4 Johnny Burnett: Nine hits in a game (July 10, 1932)

Burnett wasn't a star. In parts of nine seasons, he had only 521 career hits. Amazingly, nine of those hits came in one game, earning Burnett a spot in the record book. Burnett's Cleveland Indians and the Philadelphia Athletics needed 18 innings to settle a game that the A's eventually won 18–17, but Burnett did his part for Cleveland, smoking seven singles and two doubles in 11 at-bats.

5 Shawn Green: 19 total bases in a game (May 23, 2002)

The Dodgers rightfielder was off to a slow start in 2002, and was even benched at one point in mid-May. But he broke out in a big way later that month. In a game against the Brewers, Green came to the plate six times. He hit four home runs, a double, and a single. Green's 19 total bases set an MLB record.

6 Sandy Koufax: 14 strikeouts in a perfect game (September 9, 1965)

Of the 20 perfect games in major league history, none was more dominating than Koufax's against the Cubs. The Dodgers ace retired 27 in a row, 14 of them by strikeout, the most ever in a perfect game.

7 Fernando Tatis: Two grand slams in one inning (April 23, 1999)

The Cardinals third baseman had an inning to remember against Dodgers pitcher Chan-Ho Park. With the bases loaded in the third, Tatis blasted a pitch deep over the leftfield wall. The Cards continued to hammer Park until Tatis had another at-bat in the inning — also with the bases loaded. With the count full, he smashed a hanging breaking ball. Tatis became the only player to hit two grand slams in one inning.

8 Johnny Vander Meer: Second straight no-hitter (June 15, 1938)

The Cincinnati Reds lefty's no-hitter against the Brooklyn Dodgers wasn't just an ordinary no-no — it was Vander Meer's second one in a row. He had no-hit the Boston Braves just four days earlier. He remains the only pitcher to throw back-to-back no-hitters.

9 Mark Whiten: Four homers, 12 RBIs in a game (September 7, 1993)

After going hitless in Game 1 of a doubleheader, Whiten redeemed himself in Game 2. He came to the plate five times and slugged four homers while driving in 12 runs. He tied the record in both categories, and also tied the all-time mark for RBIs in a doubleheader, with 13. (He had a bases-loaded walk in the first game.)

10 Gary Gaetti, Al Newman, and Kent Hrbek: Two triple plays in a game (July 17, 1990)

You may know the triple-double in basketball. The Twins pulled off a baseball double-triple. With the bases loaded in the fourth inning, Red Sox cleanup hitter Tom Brunansky hit a sharp ground ball down the third-base line. Gaetti scooped it up and stepped on third for one out, gunned it for out Number 2 to Newman, who then fired it to Hrbek at first for the triple play. With runners on first and second in the eighth, it happened again. It's the only time a team has turned two triple plays in a game.

1 Mariano Rivera's cutter
Since discovering his signature pitch by accident in 1997, the New York Yankees legend has used it to become the greatest closer of all time. His cutter looks like a regular fastball until it breaks sharply to the left at the last moment.

2 Sandy Koufax's curveball
Koufax, the 1963 NL MVP and Cy Young Award winner, devastated hitters with his curveball. The Dodgers lefty threw it hard, and the pitch would start at a hitter's eyes before diving down to his knees.

3 Walter Johnson's fastball
The combination of speed and the Big Train's unusual sidearm delivery made his heater nearly untouchable. Johnson used it to win 417 games and strike out 3,508 hitters in a 21-year career with the Washington Senators (1907–27).

4 Carl Hubbell's screwball
The screwball is like a reverse curveball that moves right to left. No one threw it better than Hubbell, who won two MVP awards (1933 and '36) during a Hall of Fame career with the New York Giants.

5 Johan Santana's change-up
The change-up is about deception. When the Mets ace throws his change-up, the delivery is identical to his fastball, but the pitch comes in 12 miles per hour slower. He used his fastball–change-up combo to win two Cy Young Awards (2004, '06).

6 Hoyt Wilhelm's knuckleball
The first pitcher to master the tricky knuckler and use it almost exclusively, Wilhelm played for nine teams from 1952 to '72. By putting friction on the ball's seams, he caused the pitch to float and move in unpredictable ways.

7 Bruce Sutter's splitter
Sutter held the ball with his index and middle fingers on either side, then used pressure from his index finger to add extra spin. The result was a fastball that dove almost straight down when it reached the plate. Sutter finished his career with 300 saves and an NL Cy Young Award with the Cubs in 1979.

8 Stan Coveleski's spitball
The spitball is as gross as it sounds. Coveleski would use saliva to make a wet spot on the ball, changing the shape and weight to give it more movement. It was later made illegal, but the spitball helped him lead the AL in ERA in 1923 (while playing for the Indians) and '25 (with the Washington Senators) and earned him a spot in the Hall of Fame.

9 Randy Johnson's slider
The Big Unit's breaking ball fooled both lefty and righty hitters. A five-time Cy Young Award winner and a 2001 World Series MVP with the Diamondbacks, Johnson threw a 90 mile-per-hour slider that would seem to disappear as it dove toward the back foot of a righthanded hitter.

10 Mordecai Brown's curveball
Brown earned the nickname Three Finger because he lost most of his right index finger in a farming accident and badly hurt his middle finger later in life. But the damage done to his hand may have helped his baseball career. Brown's curve had an unusual amount of movement, allowing him to dominate hitters in the early part of the 1900s. He had a career 2.06 ERA.

Top 10
Toughest Pitches

Top 10 World Series

Moments

1 Bill Mazeroski's World Series–winning home run
1960 World Series, Game 7
Pirates vs. Yankees

Mazeroski was an eight-time Gold Glove winner as a second baseman for the Pittsburgh Pirates, but the biggest moment of his career came from an uncharacteristic surge of power at the plate. In the top of the ninth inning during Game 7 of the 1960 World Series, the New York Yankees tied the game by scoring two runs. Maz led off the bottom of the inning, and on a 1–0 count, he blasted a pitch over the leftfield wall. His home run won the World Series for the underdog Pirates. It was the first Series-ending home run in history and remains the only walk-off homer ever hit in a Game 7.

2 Joe Carter's World Series–winning home run
1993 World Series, Game 6
Blue Jays vs. Phillies

During the 1993 World Series, Carter's Toronto Blue Jays led the Philadelphia Phillies three games to two in the Series and 5–1 in the game. Philadelphia would not go down quietly. A five-run seventh inning sparked by Lenny Dykstra's three-run homer gave the Phillies a 6–5 lead in the ninth. Carter came up to bat with one out in the bottom of the inning and teammates Paul Molitor and Rickey Henderson on base. Carter ripped a 2–2 pitch over the leftfield wall to clinch the Series for the Jays. The five-time All-Star was no stranger to clutch hitting in the World Series: The previous year he had hit two home runs when the Blue Jays defeated the Braves for the title.

3 Don Larsen's perfect game
1956 World Series, Game 5
Yankees vs. Dodgers

Before Larsen, only three modern-era pitchers had thrown a perfect game. None of them did it in as high-pressured a situation as Larsen. With the 1956 World Series between the Yankees and the Brooklyn Dodgers tied at two games apiece, New York manager Casey Stengel gave the ball to Larsen despite his shaky start in Game 2. Larsen responded by completely shutting down the Dodgers' lineup, which included stars such as Roy Campanella, Jackie Robinson, and Duke Snider. With two outs in the ninth, Larsen struck out Dale Mitchell for his 27th out in 27 batters. Yankees catcher Yogi Berra leaped into Larsen's arms to celebrate what remains the only perfect game in postseason history.

4 Sandy Koufax's shutout
1965 World Series, Game 7
Dodgers vs. Yankees

Koufax missed Game 1 of the 1965 World Series against the New York Yankees because it fell on Yom Kippur, but he made up for his absence later in the Series. He bounced back from a poor Game 2 by pitching a shutout in Game 5 and, amazingly, returned on two days' rest to start Game 7. Koufax ignored a sore arm and pitched a three-hit shutout that wrapped up the Series for the Los Angeles Dodgers. After the accomplishment Koufax was named SPORTS ILLUSTRATED's Sportsman of the Year.

5 Reggie Jackson's three home runs
1977 World Series, Game 6
Yankees vs. Dodgers

Jackson earned the nickname Mr. October after showcasing his power during Game 6 of the 1977 World Series. The New York Yankees won the game 8–4 thanks to Jackson, who took three different Los Angeles Dodgers pitchers deep, in the fourth, fifth, and eighth innings. The rightfielder had also hit a home run in his final at-bat of Game 5, meaning Mr. October hit four home runs in four straight swings during the Series. Jackson's five home runs is tied for the most by one player in a single World Series.

6 Bill Buckner's error
1986 World Series, Game 6
Mets vs. Red Sox

The Curse of the Bambino infamously struck during Game 6 of the 1986 World Series. The heavily favored New York Mets trailed the Boston Red Sox three games to two in the Series and were down by two runs in the bottom of the tenth inning before a two-out rally tied the game. That's when New York's Mookie Wilson hit a slow grounder toward Boston's Buckner at first base. Buckner, slowed by injuries, feared Wilson would beat out the play at first, and rushed while fielding the ball. It went through Buckner's legs. Mets third baseman Ray Knight scored on the botched play, winning the game and forcing a Game 7. The Mets went on to win the decisive game and the Series.

8 Kirby Puckett's walk-off home run
1991 World Series, Game 6, Twins vs. Braves
The Minnesota Twins trailed the Atlanta Braves three games to two in the 1991 World Series. Luckily, the Twins had Puckett to help turn things around. In the third inning he leaped into the outfield wall to rob the Braves of a key extra-base hit. Then, with the game tied in the 11th, Puckett hit a walk-off home run. The Twins went on to win Game 7 in one of the most exciting World Series of all time.

9 Kirk Gibson's pinch-hit home run
1988 World Series, Game 1, Dodgers vs. A's
NL MVP Gibson led the Los Angeles Dodgers to the 1988 World Series. Once there, however, he was too injured to start. In Game 1, with L.A. trailing 4–3 with two outs and one man on, Gibson was called to pinch-hit in the ninth. He battled through a long at-bat against A's closer Dennis Eckersley before smacking a slider into the stands. Gibson's game-winning home run trot is legendary, as he limped around the bases pumping his fist.

7 David Freese's walk-off home run
2011 World Series, Game 6
Cardinals vs. Rangers
The St. Louis Cardinals' season appeared to be over in the ninth inning, with the Texas Rangers leading the Series three games to two and ahead by two runs. Down to his last strike, Freese slapped a two-out triple that scored two runs and sent the game into extra innings. He struck again in the 11th, slugging a walk-off home run over the centerfield wall to keep St. Louis's title hopes alive. The Cardinals went on to win Game 7, and Freese was named the World Series MVP.

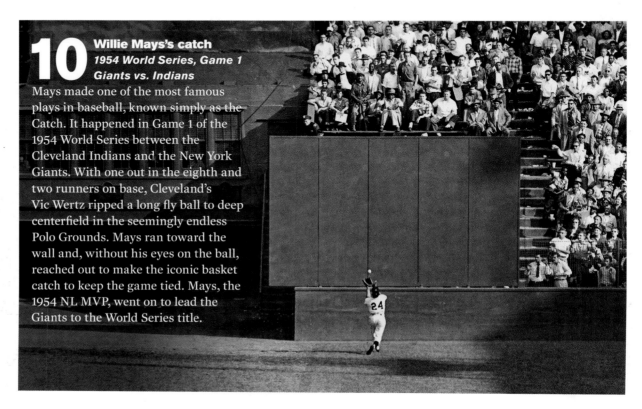

10 Willie Mays's catch
1954 World Series, Game 1
Giants vs. Indians
Mays made one of the most famous plays in baseball, known simply as the Catch. It happened in Game 1 of the 1954 World Series between the Cleveland Indians and the New York Giants. With one out in the eighth and two runners on base, Cleveland's Vic Wertz ripped a long fly ball to deep centerfield in the seemingly endless Polo Grounds. Mays ran toward the wall and, without his eyes on the ball, reached out to make the iconic basket catch to keep the game tied. Mays, the 1954 NL MVP, went on to lead the Giants to the World Series title.

TOP 10 MOST INT

1 Bob Gibson, *Pitcher*
MLB Career: 1959–75

Everything the Cardinals pitcher did had hitters shaking in their shoes. There was his scowl (he would later say he was just squinting to see the catcher's signs) and ferocious windup, but Gibson is best known for coming in high and tight. "He'd knock you down," the Phillies' Dick Allen once said, "and then meet you at home plate to see if you wanted to make something of it."

2 Ty Cobb, *Centerfielder*
MLB Career: 1905–28

Despite having the highest career batting average in baseball history, Cobb is more often known as the meanest man ever to play the game. He was aggressive on the base paths, not only daring the fielder to try to throw him out but also taunting the one waiting to make the tag on him. Cobb even sharpened his spikes for his vicious feet-first slides.

3 Willie McCovey
First Baseman
MLB Career: 1959–80

Pitcher Bob Gibson once called the 6'5", 210-pound McCovey "the scariest hitter in baseball." When McCovey got ahold of a pitch, there was no doubt it was leaving the park. Managers didn't intentionally walk hitters as often as they do now, and McCovey's 45 intentional walks in 1969, while playing for the Giants, was a record that stood for 33 seasons.

4 Dick Radatz, *Pitcher*
MLB Career: 1962–69

Radatz faced Mickey Mantle 67 times in his career and struck him out 44 times, leading the Yankees legend to give Radatz his nickname, The Monster. At 6'5", 235 pounds, Radatz was the original power closer. After a slow windup came a 95-mile-per-hour fastball that exploded past hitters. He holds the single-season mark for strikeouts by a reliever (181 in 1964).

5 Willie Stargell
Leftfielder/First Baseman
MLB Career: 1962–82

Stargell struck fear into pitchers with his moonshot home runs. A leader of the Pittsburgh Pirates during their 1970s heyday, he hit 475 career home runs on his way to the Hall of Fame. He also sent a message before the pitch came in. Stargell often swung a sledgehammer in the on-deck circle and spun his bat at the pitcher during the windup.

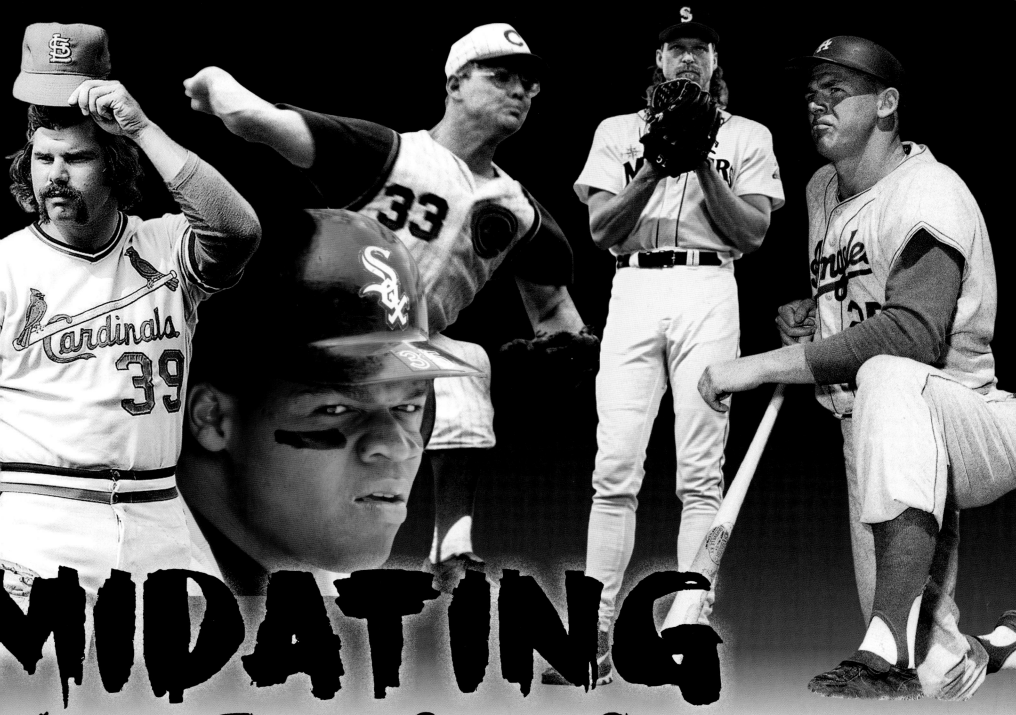

MIDATING

6 **Al Hrabosky,** *Pitcher*
MLB Career: 1970–82
Hrabosky didn't earn the nickname The Mad Hungarian for nothing. He had a ridiculously overgrown mustache and a crazed look in his eye when he stared in at hitters. Undersized at 5'11" and with only average stuff, he relied as much on style as he did on talent. His attitude was a big reason he was able to pile up an NL-leading 22 saves for the Cardinals in 1975.

7 **Frank Thomas**
First Baseman/DH
MLB Career: 1990–2008
When opposing pitchers looked at the 6' 5", 275-pound Thomas, they'd see a guy who crowded the plate and was so big that a bat looked like a twig in his hands. In his 19-year career (16 of them with the White Sox), The Big Hurt hit 521 home runs. Pitchers were so scared to pitch to Thomas that he drew 1,667 walks in his career, 10th most of all time.

8 **Ryne Duren,** *Pitcher*
MLB Career: 1954–65
There's nothing scarier than a guy who throws a 100-mile-per-hour fastball — unless it's a guy who throws one and has no idea where it's going. A big journeyman reliever with thick glasses, Duren kept hitters on their toes. He struck out more than a batter per inning during his career, but he also had one of the highest walk rates in major league history.

9 **Randy Johnson**
Pitcher
MLB Career: 1988–2009
When the 6'10" Johnson threw his fastball, it looked as if he was unleashing it from three feet in front of the plate. In the 1993 All-Star Game, a pitch slipped out of his hand and sailed over the head of the Phillies' John Kruk. Kruk was so scared that he barely stepped back into the batter's box. He looked genuinely relieved when he finally struck out.

10 **Frank Howard**
Outfielder
MLB Career: 1958–73
Known as The Capital Punisher, Howard, who stood at 6' 8" and 255 pounds, menaced pitchers every time he stepped up to the plate. He was a great athlete — Howard was also drafted to play in the NBA — who packed a ton of power. Howard hit 382 career home runs, including 44 or more in three straight seasons from 1968 to '70.

Top 10 Man

1 **John McGraw**
Managing Career: 1899–1932

McGraw was a great player, hitting .334 and scoring 1,024 runs over a 16-year career. But he was an even better manager. Known as Little Napoleon for the way he ruled over his teams, McGraw won 10 National League pennants and three World Series with the New York Giants. He ranks second all time with 2,763 managerial victories.

2 **Casey Stengel**
Managing Career: 1934–36, '38–43, '49–60, '62–65

Stengel, who earned the nickname Old Perfessor for his smarts, helmed some of the greatest Yankees teams of all time, leading them to five straight World Series (1949 to '53). He won a total of seven championships with the Bronx Bombers, tied for the most ever by a manager, before ending his career across town with the newly formed Mets.

3 **Connie Mack**
Managing Career: 1894–96, 1901–50

Mack managed in the big leagues for 53 years, including a half century with the Philadelphia Athletics. Over that time, he won 3,731 games (almost 1,000 more than John McGraw, who has the second most) and five World Series titles. Mack was known for being an even-tempered manager who sat in the dugout in a suit as opposed to a baseball uniform.

4 **Joe McCarthy**
Managing Career: 1926–46, '48–50

One of the few Hall of Fame managers to have never played in the big leagues, McCarthy had a .615 career winning percentage, the highest among all skippers who managed at least 320 games. McCarthy won seven championships with the great Yankees teams of the 1930s and '40s, which featured legends such as Babe Ruth, Lou Gehrig, and Joe DiMaggio.

5 **Tony La Russa**
Managing Career: 1979–2011

La Russa exited the game on top. He retired in 2011 after leading the Cardinals to an improbable World Series triumph. La Russa won two championships in St. Louis and one in Oakland. He and Sparky Anderson are the only managers to win the World Series in both leagues. La Russa ranks third all time with 2,728 managerial victories.

agers

6 **Joe Torre**
Managing Career: 1977–84, '90–2010

To overshadow his playing career, which included nine All-Star Games and an MVP award, Torre needed to be one heck of a manager. And he was. Torre managed the Yankees dynasty of the late 1990s. His '98 squad was one of the best in history, winning 114 games during the regular season and sweeping the Padres in the World Series.

7 **Walter Alston**
Managing Career: 1954–76

In 1955, Alston and the Brooklyn Dodgers engineered one of the greatest World Series upsets in history, defeating the seemingly invincible Yankees in seven games to win the franchise's first championship. Alston would go on to win three more titles with the Dodgers, all of which came after the team moved to Los Angeles.

8 **Sparky Anderson**
Managing Career: 1970–95

Anderson was the mastermind behind Cincinnati's Big Red Machine teams of the 1970s, which won two World Series. His aggressive use of the bullpen is still a model for today's managers. After leaving the Reds in '78, he managed the Tigers for 17 years, taking home another title in '84 to become the first manager to win a championship in both leagues.

9 **Bobby Cox**
Managing Career: 1978–85, '90–2010

Cox was the skipper during one of the most impressive streaks in baseball history. His Braves teams made the playoffs for 14 straight seasons, between 1991 and 2005, winning five NL pennants and one World Series. Cox was never afraid to make his opinion heard on the field: He ranks first all time in game ejections (158), all as a manager.

10 **Earl Weaver**
Managing Career: 1968–82, '85–86

Weaver's fiery personality and strategy of "pitching, defense, and the three-run homer" helped make Baltimore a model franchise during his time as manager. Under his watchful eye, the Orioles won 100 games in a season five times, including three in a row from 1969 to '71. Weaver also led Baltimore to four AL pennants and a World Series title in 1970.

Double Play Combos

1 Lou Whitaker and Alan Trammell
Detroit Tigers, 1977–95

Tigers pitchers were in luck when they had the dynamic duo of second baseman Whitaker *(far left)* and shortstop Trammell *(near left)* behind them. The two combined for more than 1,300 double plays during their 19 seasons manning the middle infield together. They led Detroit to two playoffs and one World Series title, combining for 11 All-Star appearances.

2 Nellie Fox and Luis Aparicio
Chicago White Sox, 1956–62

Fox *(below, right)* and Aparicio *(below, left)* were the first middle-infield teammates to win Gold Gloves in the same season (1959 and '60). In seven seasons in Chicago, they combined for 11 All-Star appearances. Shortstop Aparicio was the Rookie of the Year in 1956, and second baseman Fox won the American League MVP in 1959, the same season the duo helped Chicago win the AL pennant. Both were elected to the Hall of Fame, and today bronze statues of Fox flipping a ball to Aparicio stand outside the White Sox's U.S. Cellular Field.

HERR

SMITH

3 Tom Herr and Ozzie Smith
St. Louis Cardinals, 1982–88

With second baseman Herr and shortstop Smith patrolling the infield together, the Cardinals went to three World Series, winning one. Few balls hit up the middle got past these guys, who also helped set the table for the Cardinals' offense, scoring 958 runs during their time together in St. Louis.

ALOMAR

VIZQUEL

7 Roberto Alomar and Omar Vizquel
Cleveland Indians, 1999–2001

In just three seasons together, these two established themselves as one of the slickest fielding combinations ever. Hall of Fame second baseman Alomar and shortstop Vizquel averaged nearly 92 double plays per season in Cleveland, and both won Gold Gloves in all three seasons they played together.

8 Dick Green and Bert Campaneris
Kansas City/Oakland A's, 1964–74

In a decade of sharing the field, this duo converted more than 700 double plays. Shortstop Campaneris *(above, left)* led the league in steals six times and finished his career with six All-Star selections. Green *(above, right)* was as sure-handed as they come at second base, finishing his career with a .983 fielding percentage.

MORGAN

CONCEPCION

9 Joe Morgan and Dave Concepcion
Cincinnati Reds, 1972–79

The Reds went to three World Series, winning two of them, with Morgan and Concepcion turning two up the middle. Second baseman Morgan won two MVPs playing next to Concepcion. The duo combined for 14 All-Star appearances and 10 Gold Gloves.

4 Chase Utley and Jimmy Rollins
Philadelphia Phillies, 2003–present

Through 2011, neither second baseman Utley *(near left)* nor shortstop Rollins *(far left)* has had a fielding percentage lower than .977 in a season. And they are just as dangerous a combination at the plate. In 2006, they became the first pair of NL middle infielders to each hit 25 home runs in a season. The Phillies have made the playoffs in five of the nine seasons the duo has played together.

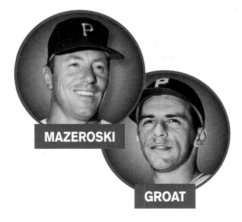

MAZEROSKI

GROAT

5 Bill Mazeroski and Dick Groat
Pittsburgh Pirates, 1956–62

Mazeroski is best known for hitting the only Game 7 walk-off home run in World Series history, but his fielding at second base was just as legendary. Mazeroski and shortstop Groat combined for seven All-Star appearances. Groat led the National League in batting average (.325) during his MVP season in 1960.

6 Davey Lopes and Bill Russell
Los Angeles Dodgers, 1973–81

The Dodgers had the same infield for eight and a half seasons (with Steve Garvey at first, Lopes at second, Russell at short, and Ron Cey at third), the longest a unit has stayed together in major league history. Lopes *(below, right)* and Russell *(below, left)* both started in the 1980 All-Star Game, held at their home stadium. They also helped the Dodgers win the World Series in 1981.

10 Robinson Cano and Derek Jeter
New York Yankees, 2005–present

Cano *(far right)* won a Gold Glove at second with Jeter *(left)* by his side at short in 2010. Cano's relaxed playing style starts some of the smoothest double plays in baseball, but things are much more explosive at the plate for these two. From 2005 to '11, Cano and Jeter combined for 234 home runs and more than 1,100 RBIs to lead the Yankees to six playoff appearances and one World Series title. They helped the Yankees turn an AL-best 151 double plays in 2007.

1 Ken Griffey Jr. and Ken Griffey Sr.

On September 14, 1990, in the first inning against the California Angels, Seattle Mariners leftfielder Ken Sr. smashed a home run over the fence in left centerfield. His son Ken Jr. congratulated him at home plate — and then hit a long ball to the same spot. The Griffeys became the only father-son duo in major league history to hit back-to-back homers. The tandem played two seasons together before the elder Griffey retired in 1991. Ken Sr. was a three-time All-Star who won two World Series titles with the Reds. Ken Jr., the 1997 AL MVP, became a member of the 600–home run club in 2008.

2 Prince and Cecil Fielder

When Prince signed with the Detroit Tigers in 2012, the first baseman returned to the Motor City, where his dad, Cecil, was a star slugger. Cecil led the American League in home runs and RBIs in 1990 (51 homers, 132 RBIs) and '91 (44, 133). Prince inherited his dad's big bat. A three-time All-Star, Prince hit a National League–best 50 homers with the Milwaukee Brewers in 2007.

Top 10 Fam

6 Joe and Phil Niekro

The two starting pitchers have a combined 539 wins, making them the winningest brothers on the mound. Pitching for the Houston Astros in 1979, Joe led the NL with 21 wins and five shutouts. Phil, a five-time Gold Glove winner, threw a no-hitter in 1973 for the Atlanta Braves.

7 Vince, Joe, and Dom DiMaggio

All three brothers were stars in centerfield. Oldest brother Vince was a two-time All-Star with the Pittsburgh Pirates. Joe, a three-time AL MVP for the New York Yankees, won nine World Series titles. Youngest brother Dom hit over .300 four times in 10 full seasons with the Boston Red Sox.

3 Sandy Jr., Sandy Sr., and Roberto Alomar

"Everything I learned about the game of baseball, I learned from my dad," Roberto, a 10-time Gold Glove–winning second baseman, said when he was inducted into the Baseball Hall of Fame in 2011. Older brother Sandy Jr., an All-Star catcher, also looked up to Sandy Sr., who had a 15-year career as a second baseman.

ies

4 Cal Sr., Cal Jr., and Billy Ripken

A respected coach and manager during his 36 years in the Baltimore Orioles organization, Cal Sr. managed both of his sons in 1987. Cal Jr. famously played a major-league-record 2,632 consecutive games. The 1982 Rookie of the Year also won the American League MVP twice and was named an All-Star 19 times in his 21 seasons as Baltimore's shortstop and third baseman. Younger brother Billy, who also played for the Rangers, Indians, and Tigers, had a 12-year career as an infielder.

5 Felipe, Matty, and Jesus Alou

Playing for the San Francisco Giants, the brothers were the first set of siblings to play the outfield together when they took the field in the eighth inning of a game on September 15, 1963. Oldest brother Felipe, a three-time All-Star, finished with 2,101 hits in 17 seasons. (His son, Moises, would become a six-time All-Star.) Middle brother Matty, the 1966 NL batting champion, hit .307 for his career. Jesus, the youngest brother, was a career .280 hitter who won World Series titles with the Oakland A's in 1973 and '74.

10 B.J. and Justin Upton

The Uptons are the highest-drafted siblings of all time — older brother B.J. was selected second overall by the Tampa Bay Devil Rays in 2002, and little brother Justin was taken by the Arizona Diamondbacks with the top pick in 2005. They're already both members of the 20–20 club (hitting 20 home runs and stealing 20 bases in a season).

8 Pedro and Ramon Martinez

The two flamethrowing brothers had successful careers on the mound and briefly played together with the Los Angeles Dodgers and the Boston Red Sox. Younger brother Pedro, a three-time Cy Young Award winner, became a World Series champion in 2004 with Boston. Ramon, who had a career 135–88 record, pitched a no-hitter in 1995.

9 Paul and Lloyd Waner

The Waners are the only brothers to both be inducted in the Hall of Fame. They hold the career record for hits by brothers (5,611) and patrolled the outfield together for the Pittsburgh Pirates for 14 seasons. Paul, nicknamed Big Poison, was a career .333 hitter and won the 1927 National League MVP award. Lloyd, known as Little Poison, was a career .316 hitter. He batted .400 in the 1927 World Series.

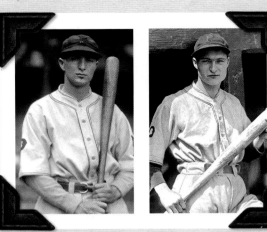

Top 10 Minor League Team Names

1 **Richmond (Virginia) Flying Squirrels**
Fans suggested the nickname for the San Francisco Giants' Double A affiliate in 2009. The team's popular mascot is a caped squirrel called Nutzy.

2 **Montgomery (Alabama) Biscuits**
Evan Longoria played third base for the Tampa Bay Rays' Double A team with the tasty name.

3 **Jamestown (New York) Jammers**
The A ball team of the Miami Marlins has a name that honors the region's grape-growing.

4 **Lehigh Valley (Pennsylvania) IronPigs**
The Philadelphia Phillies' Triple A squad has two mascots: Ferrous and FeFe, named after the chemical name and abbreviation for iron.

5 **Fort Wayne (Indiana) TinCaps**
The A ball team of the San Diego Padres has a name inspired by folk hero Johnny Appleseed, who was known for wearing a tin pot on his head.

6 **Toledo (Ohio) Mud Hens**
In the late 1800s, the Detroit Tigers' Triple A affiliate played in a marsh that was populated by birds called coots, which are also known as mud hens.

7 **Omaha (Nebraska) Storm Chasers**
The Kansas City Royals' Triple A team is a nod to the unpredictable weather in Nebraska.

8 **Albuquerque (New Mexico) Isotopes**
The Triple A squad for the Los Angeles Dodgers gets its nickname from the fictional baseball team on *The Simpsons*.

9 **Asheville (North Carolina) Tourists**
Named after the visitors who love exploring western North Carolina, the Colorado Rockies' A ball affiliate got its nickname in 1914.

10 **Savannah (Georgia) Sand Gnats**
The New York Mets' A ball team is named for the pesky bugs found on Georgia's coast.

TOP 10 SWITCH-HITTERS

1 Mickey Mantle, *Centerfielder, MLB Career: 1951–68*
Named after Hall of Fame catcher Mickey Cochrane, Mantle was destined for greatness. The farm boy from Commerce, Oklahoma, had both power and speed, and was dangerous from both sides of the plate. He has the highest career slugging percentage among switch-hitters (.557) and the most home runs (536). Mantle had 1,509 RBIs over an 18-year career with the Yankees, winning three MVP awards and the 1956 AL Triple Crown.

2 Pete Rose, *Outfielder/Infielder, MLB Career: 1963–86*
Baseball's hit king — Rose holds the major league record with 4,256 career hits — is also one of the most accomplished switch-hitters of all time. Charlie Hustle holds the record for most runs by a switch-hitter (2,165) and is tied for most hits by a switch-hitter in a season (230 in 1973).

3 Chipper Jones, *Third Baseman, MLB Career: 1993–present*
A natural righty, the Atlanta Braves third baseman is equally strong from both sides of the plate. Through 2011, he hit .304 as a righty and .304 as a lefty. Jones also packs some punch — he holds the NL record for career home runs by a switch-hitter (454 through 2011).

4 Eddie Murray, *First Baseman, MLB Career: 1977–97*
A switch-hitter as a kid, Murray was a righthanded batter in the minors until he started batting both ways to break out of a slump. In his first at-bat as a lefty, he doubled, and he never looked back. Murray became the only switch-hitter, and one of only four major leaguers, to reach 3,000 hits and 500 home runs.

5 Frankie Frisch, *Second Baseman, MLB Career: 1919–37*
Frisch had a strange hitting style, holding the bat cross-handed — left hand on top of the right when batting righty. Despite the unconventional grip, he had a career batting average of .316, the highest mark among switch-hitters. Frisch also held the record for most hits by a switch-hitter (2,880) until Pete Rose passed him in 1977.

6 Lance Berkman, *Outfielder/First Baseman, MLB Career: 1999–present*
Berkman has homered from both sides of the plate in a game four times in his career. Through 2011, he ranked fourth in career home runs for switch-hitters (358) and second in slugging (.545) and on-base percentage (.409).

7 Roberto Alomar, *Second Baseman, MLB Career: 1988–2004*
A slick-fielding second baseman, Alomar was just as valuable at the plate. The Hall of Famer finished his career with a .300 batting average and 4,018 total bases (both of which are fifth-best among switch-hitters). Alomar threw righthanded but had more power from the left side of the plate, hitting 142 of his 210 career homers as a lefty.

8 Cool Papa Bell, *Centerfielder, Negro Leagues Career: 1922–46*
Bell began his career as a lefthanded pitcher but soon established himself as a switch-hitting outfielder. He regularly hit better than .300 in more than two decades in the Negro Leagues. Even though he was never allowed to play in the major leagues because of his race, the Hall of Famer is regarded as one of the fastest men ever to play the game.

9 Bernie Williams, *Centerfielder, MLB Career: 1991–2006*
One of the keys to the Yankees dynasty of the late 1990s, Williams was exceptional in the postseason. He has the most playoff home runs among switch-hitters (22). He also holds overall postseason records for RBIs (80) and extra base hits (51). In Game 3 of the 1995 AL Division Series, Williams became the first player to homer from both sides of the plate in the playoffs.

10 Tim Raines, *Leftfielder, MLB Career: 1979–2002*
The man nicknamed Rock was solid from both sides of the plate: He hit .295 as a lefty and .290 as a righty. When he got on base, he caused havoc with his speed — Raines leads all major league switch-hitters in career stolen bases (808).

TOP 10 BASEBALL

1 Field of Dreams

"If you build it, he will come," whispers a voice in this classic baseball movie starring Kevin Costner and James Earl Jones. Ray Kinsella (Costner) is inspired to create a baseball diamond in the cornfields of his Iowa farm. The field turns out to be a magical place where Kinsella meets baseball legends such as Shoeless Joe Jackson.

MOVIES

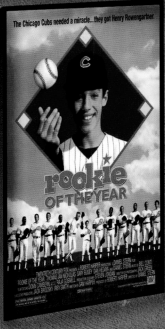

2 Angels in the Outfield
When a boy (Joseph Gordon-Levitt) who has lost his mother prays for a new family and a championship for the California Angels, he sets in motion an unlikely chain of events.

3 A League of Their Own
The all-star trio of Tom Hanks, Geena Davis, and Madonna brings big laughs in this account of the first women's pro baseball league.

4 Moneyball
This Oscar-nominated film tells the true story of how Oakland A's general manager Billy Beane (Brad Pitt) used unconventional stats to assemble an underdog playoff team.

5 The Natural
Robert Redford stars as Roy Hobbs, a player who comes out of nowhere to become the best hitter in the league by using a bat carved out of wood from a lightning-struck tree.

6 Rookie of the Year
A 12-year-old lives out his wildest dreams when a freak accident gives him the ability to throw more than 100 miles per hour, leading to a job as a pitcher with the Chicago Cubs.

7 The Pride of the Yankees
This well-regarded classic recounts the triumphant and tragic story of New York Yankees legend Lou Gehrig. Slugger Babe Ruth plays himself in the movie.

8 Eight Men Out
Told through the point of view of Chicago White Sox infielder Buck Weaver (John Cusack), this is a gripping dramatization of baseball's most notorious scandal: the 1919 White Sox team that purposely lost the World Series in exchange for money.

9 The Sandlot
A mismatched pickup baseball team gathers to play ball during a summer full of unpredictable triumphs and wacky characters.

10 Mr. 3000
Bernie Mac is hilarious as a legendary baseball hero who decides to come out of retirement to try for his 3,000th career hit.

TOP 10 SPEEDS

Rickey Henderson
Leftfielder
MLB Career: 1979–2003

An All-America running back at Oakland Technical High School, Henderson was selected by the A's in the fourth round of the 1976 draft. In 1980, his second major league season, he became only the third player in the modern era to steal 100 bases. Nicknamed the Man of Steal, Henderson kept tearing up the base paths. He reached the 100-steal mark two more times: a modern-day major-league-record 130 in 1982 and 108 in '83. He finished his career as the all-time leader in runs scored (2,295) and stolen bases (1,406). A big reason why Henderson was able to showcase his speed was due to his skill with the bat. He ranks 22nd in career hits (3,055).

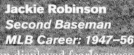

Jackie Robinson
Second Baseman
MLB Career: 1947–56
Robinson displayed fearlessness and confidence in becoming the majors' first African-American player. He showed those same qualities on the base paths. The Brooklyn Dodgers great scored more than 100 runs in six of his 10 seasons. As a rookie he led the NL in steals and earned baseball's first Rookie of the Year award. He was so sure of his speed, in fact, that he stole home 19 times in his career, including once in Game 1 of the 1955 World Series. Robinson also led the league in steals and batting average in 1949 and was named NL MVP.

2 Lou Brock
Leftfielder, MLB Career: 1961–79
One of the best all-around players ever, Brock used his speed to beat out grounders, steal bases, and run down balls in the gap. Brock's 938 career stolen bases rank second behind Rickey Henderson, and he also won the National League stolen-base title eight times. It's no wonder that today the NL player who finishes the season with the most steals receives the Lou Brock Award. The Hall of Famer also hit better than .300 eight times during his career with the Cardinals, won two World Series titles, and is a member of the 3,000-hit club.

3 Cool Papa Bell
Outfielder, Negro Leagues
Career: 1922–46
Legendary pitcher Satchel Paige once said Cool Papa Bell was so fast, "he could turn off the light and be under the covers before the room gets dark!" Bell once scored from first on an infield bunt, and he also stole two bases on one pitch. It's even rumored that he could round the bases in 12 seconds.

6 Vince Coleman
Leftfielder, MLB Career: 1985–97
Coleman hit the ground running: During his rookie season with the Cardinals, in 1985, he finished with a National League–best 110 steals (the third-highest single-season total in the modern era). The feat helped him earn the NL Rookie of the Year award. Coleman was just getting started. He went on to lead the NL in steals for six straight seasons. Coleman reached 500 steals in only 804 games, faster than any other player, and ranks sixth on the all-time steals list.

7 Deion Sanders
Centerfielder
MLB Career: 1989–95, '97, 2001
The only man to play in both a World Series and a Super Bowl, Prime Time gave new meaning to the term *flashy player*. He was like a bolt of lightning on the base paths but never played a full season because of his football commitments. As a member of the Atlanta Braves in 1992, Sanders led the NL with 14 triples despite missing the last part of the regular season to attend NFL training camp.

5 Willie Wilson
Outfielder
MLB Career: 1976–94

You need to have wheels to hit 13 inside-the-park home runs during your career. Wilson, who won the American League batting title in 1982, led the league in stolen bases as a member of the Royals in 1979. The following season he hit .326 and led the AL in runs (133), hits (230), and triples (15). Catchers didn't stand much of a chance of throwing Wilson out on the base paths — he finished his career with a stolen-base percentage of 83.3.

8 Maury Wills
Shortstop
MLB Career: 1959–72

Not only did Wills steal more bases than any other player while playing for the Dodgers in 1962, his 104 steals were more than any other *team*. Wills also hit 10 triples, earning him the NL MVP award that season. He had the most steals in the NL for six straight years and hit 71 triples in his career.

9 Carl Crawford
Leftfielder
MLB Career: 2002–present

In May 2009, Crawford stole six bases in a single game, tying a modern-era record. He is a four-time AL stolen-base champion, and through 2011, his 112 triples are the most of any active big leaguer. In 2010 he became the second player to hit 100 triples and steal 400 bases before turning age 30.

10 Dave Roberts
Outfielder, MLB Career: 1999–2008

While Roberts was always considered one of the better base stealers in baseball during his 10-year career, he became an instant hero thanks to his performance in Game 4 of the 2004 ALCS. With the Red Sox trailing the Yankees 4–3 in the ninth inning of an elimination game, Roberts pinch-ran at first base. Yankees closer Mariano Rivera attempted to pick Roberts off three times, but the fearless speedster eventually took off for second and beat out the throw. Roberts then scored from second on a single, and the Red Sox won the game in 12 innings. The Sox went on to win the ALCS in seven games on their way to their first World Series title since 1918.

TOP 10 "Yogi

With 10 World Series rings, New York Yankees Hall of Fame catcher **Yogi Berra** knows a thing or two about baseball and life. Here are some of the wise (and funny) words that are credited to Yogi.

1

"Ninety percent of this game is half mental."

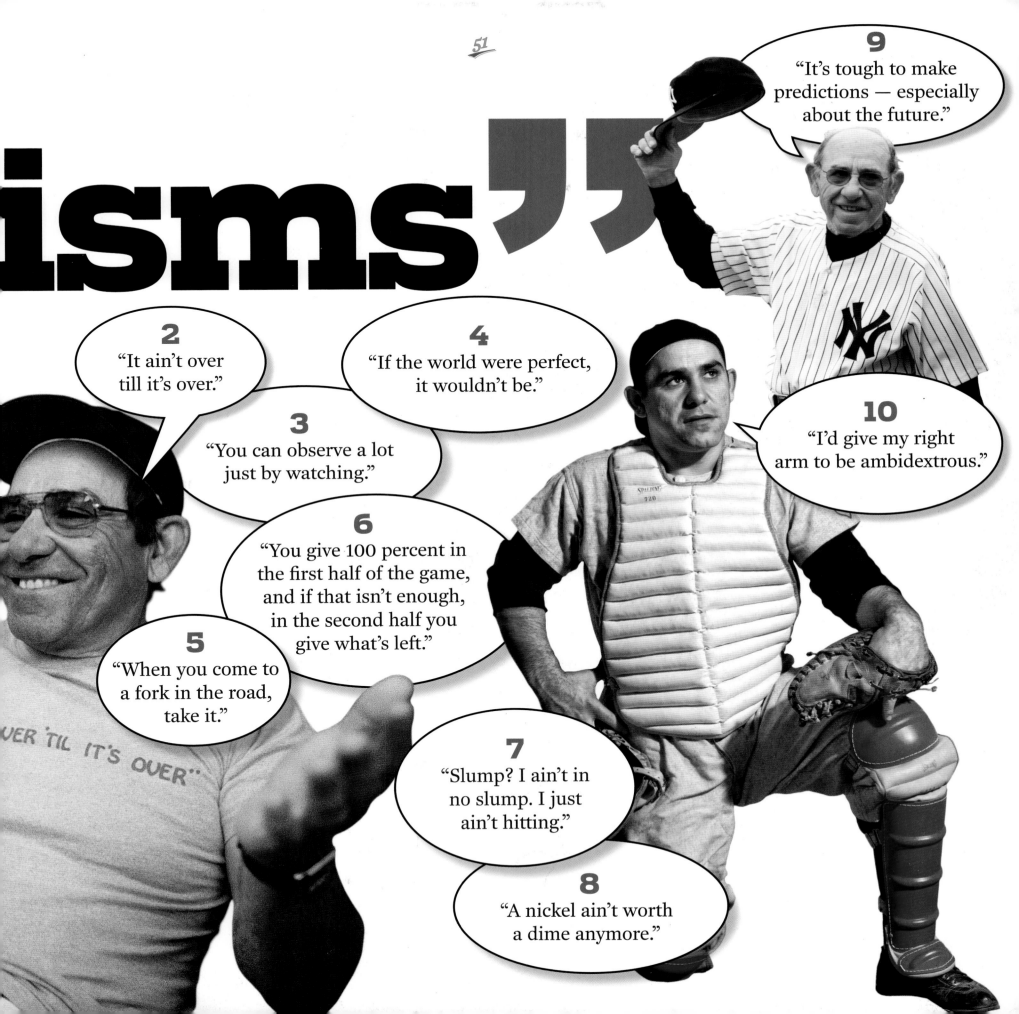

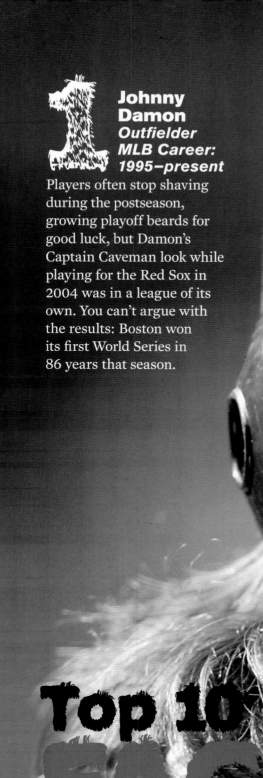

Johnny Damon
Outfielder
MLB Career:
1995–present

Players often stop shaving during the postseason, growing playoff beards for good luck, but Damon's Captain Caveman look while playing for the Red Sox in 2004 was in a league of its own. You can't argue with the results: Boston won its first World Series in 86 years that season.

Top 10 FACIAL HAIR

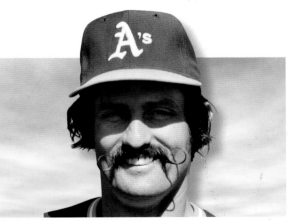

2 Rollie Fingers
Pitcher, MLB Career: 1968–85
In 1972, Oakland A's owner Charles Finley offered $300 to any team member who started the season sporting a mustache. Fingers grew a handlebar mustache, which became his signature look.

3 Brian Wilson
Pitcher, MLB Career: 2006–present
Wilson's FEAR THE BEARD campaign really worked. Since he grew out his beard and dyed it black in 2010, the Giants closer has earned two All-Star selections and a World Series trophy.

4 Scott Spiezio
Infielder, MLB Career: 1996–2007
Spiezio's red-dyed soul patch was such a hit during St. Louis's 2006 World Series championship season that Cardinals fans could buy replicas of it outside Busch Stadium.

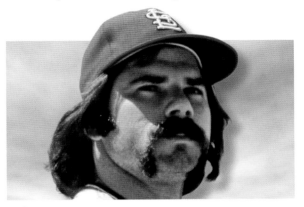

5 Al Hrabosky
Pitcher, MLB Career: 1970–82
Hrabosky credited his Fu Manchu for his solid pitching in St. Louis. In 1976, when new Cardinals manager Vern Rapp banned facial hair, the clean-cut Hrabosky had some of the worst numbers of his career.

6 David Ortiz
Designated Hitter, MLB Career: 1997–present
Big Papi likes to change up his look while shaving. The Red Sox slugger is rarely seen without a uniquely designed, carefully carved chin strap.

7 John Axford
Pitcher, MLB Career: 2009–present
Even though he is Canadian, the Brewers closer was named the 2011 Robert Goulet Memorial Mustached American of the Year by the American Mustache Institute.

8 Bobby Jenks
Pitcher, MLB Career: 2005–present
On Mother's Day in 2008, Jenks gave his bleach-blond goatee an even more striking look when he dyed it pink to support breast cancer awareness.

9 Dustin Hermanson
Pitcher, MLB Career: 1995–2006
Hermanson, who played for six organizations in 12 seasons, created works of art with his goatee, shaving geometric designs into his facial hair.

10 Eddie Murray
First Baseman, MLB Career: 1977–97
Steady Eddie cut his stylish sideburns in the late 1980s, but a well-groomed mustache was the Hall of Fame switch-hitter's trademark until he retired in 1997.

Top 10
Future
Hall of Fa

1 Albert Pujols
First Baseman

In the ninth inning of Game 3 of the 2011 World Series, Pujols sent a moon shot into leftfield. The slugger had smacked many long balls in his career, but that home run, his third of the night, put him in the record books. He became the third player, after Yankees legends Babe Ruth and Reggie Jackson, to hit three homers in a World Series game. It was just the latest addition to Pujols's long list of baseball accomplishments. In his first 11 big-league seasons, all with the St. Louis Cardinals, Pujols won three National League MVP awards and two World Series and made the All-Star team nine times. He signed with the Los Angeles Angels before 2012 and entered the season as a career .328 hitter, averaging 42 home runs and 126 RBIs per season. With plenty of good years ahead of him, Pujols could go down as the greatest righthanded hitter of all time.

mers

2 Derek Jeter
Shortstop

It's hard to believe now, but before Jeter's rookie year, the Yankees had gone 14 years without winning a playoff series, and 18 years without a World Series win. With Captain Jeter lining hit after hit at the top of the order (his 3,088 career hits through 2011 led all active players), the Bronx Bombers won five World Series from 1996 to 2009.

3 Ichiro Suzuki
Rightfielder

Ichiro operates with precision at the plate and is difficult to catch on the base paths. After playing for nine seasons in the Japanese baseball league, he came to the Seattle Mariners and immediately dominated. Ichiro finished with 200 or more hits in a record 10 consecutive major league seasons. He also possesses a rocket arm, making him one of the greatest all-around outfielders ever to play the game.

4 Mariano Rivera
Relief Pitcher

After beginning his career as a starter, Rivera has become the greatest closer in major league history. He is the majors' career saves leader (603 through 2011) and has also saved more than twice as many playoff games (42) as any other pitcher ever in the big leagues. Rivera is a 12-time All-Star and has helped the Yankees win five World Series championships.

5 Roy Halladay
Starting Pitcher

Halladay is one of only five pitchers to win a Cy Young Award in both the American and National Leagues. In 2010, the 6' 6" righthander completed a perfect game and was the second pitcher ever to throw a no-hitter in the postseason. His pinpoint control and mental toughness have led to three 20-win seasons and eight All-Star Game appearances through 2011.

6 Vladimir Guerrero
Rightfielder

One of the most feared sluggers in modern-day baseball, Guerrero in his prime had the rare ability to drive any pitch — no matter how far outside the strike zone. The 2004 American League MVP has made nine All-Star teams and has had 100-RBI seasons for three franchises (the Montreal Expos, the Los Angeles Angels, and the Texas Rangers).

7 CC Sabathia
Starting Pitcher

Sabathia was only 20 years old when he made his big-league debut for the Cleveland Indians in 2001. He won 17 games that year. Since then, the supersized (6' 7", 290 pounds) southpaw has established himself as one of baseball's true aces. Just 31 years old entering the 2012 season and already with 176 career victories, he's one of the few active pitchers with a shot at 300 wins.

9 Ivan Rodriguez
Catcher

One of the greatest defensive catchers of all time, Rodriguez had a cannon of an arm. He led the American League in percentage of runners caught stealing nine times. Rodriguez broke into the big leagues as a teenager and steadily developed into an offensive force as well. He was selected to 10 consecutive All-Star Games for the Rangers (1992–2001) and was the AL MVP in 1999.

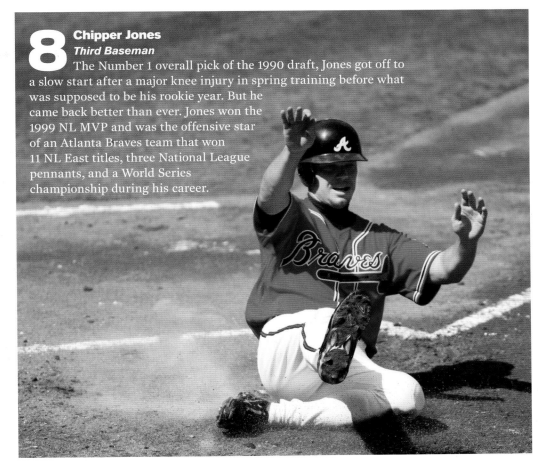

8 **Chipper Jones**
Third Baseman
The Number 1 overall pick of the 1990 draft, Jones got off to a slow start after a major knee injury in spring training before what was supposed to be his rookie year. But he came back better than ever. Jones won the 1999 NL MVP and was the offensive star of an Atlanta Braves team that won 11 NL East titles, three National League pennants, and a World Series championship during his career.

10 **Jim Thome**
First Baseman
Thome's mighty lefthanded swing has made him one of the most feared hitters of the past 20 years. That's a big reason why he is one of the eight members of the 600-home-run club and has also drawn the eighth-most walks in MLB history (1,725 through 2011). Thome is also one of only 58 players with a career on-base percentage higher than .400 (minimum of 3,000 plate appearances).

TOP 10
SCANDALS

The 1919 Chicago White Sox

One of the biggest disappointments in sports history was the incident known as the Black Sox Scandal. The Chicago White Sox were heavily favored to beat the Cincinnati Reds in the 1919 World Series. But, unhappy with team management, numerous key players made a deal with gamblers to lose the Series on purpose in exchange for a share of the gambling profits. They were eventually found out, and prior to the 1921 season, commissioner Kenesaw Mountain Landis banned eight White Sox players from baseball.

2 The Steroid Era

Some of baseball's most famous records, such as career home runs and homers in a season, fell during the 1990s and 2000s, but those marks have come under scrutiny. That's because numerous players were found to have used performance-enhancing drugs during those years. Many feel that the marks broken during this era should have asterisks in the record book.

3 Pete Rose's gambling

Rose has more hits than anyone in major league baseball history. But the hit king is not in the Hall of Fame and has been banned from baseball since 1989. Rose was caught betting on Cincinnati Reds games when he was the team's manager. He has applied for reinstatement multiple times, and has been denied every time.

4 Gaylord Perry's spitball

Perry became famous for throwing a spitball, a pitch that had been outlawed more than 40 years before his rookie season in 1962. In addition to using saliva, he allegedly doctored balls with Vaseline that he put on the zipper of his pants, thinking umpires would not check there. Perry didn't get caught until the 21st season of his Hall of Fame career.

5 Albert Belle's corked bat

Belle, a slugger for the Cleveland Indians, had the most creative cover-up when he was caught cheating. During a 1994 game in Chicago, the opposing White Sox asked the umpires to take a closer look at Belle's bat *(below)*. The bat was sent to the umpire's office for investigation. Belle and the Indians knew it was corked, so Cleveland reliever Jason Grimsley took a flashlight down to the clubhouse and climbed through the air vents, dropping down from the ceiling of the umpire's room. He took Belle's bat, replaced it with a non-corked bat, then crawled back to the clubhouse. The spy moves were later discovered, and Belle was suspended for seven games.

6 The New York Giants' stolen signs

In 2001, a *Wall Street Journal* article revealed that the 1951 Giants, who won the National League pennant with third baseman Bobby Thomson's famous walk-off home run against the Brooklyn Dodgers, may have stolen pitching signs. The Giants allegedly had an elaborate system in which a spy would watch the opposing catcher's signs through a telescope from a team office above the centerfield wall at New York's Polo Grounds. He would relay the pitch with a buzzer that went off in the dugout and the bullpen. Then, a team member would supposedly tip off the batter.

7 Joe Niekro's hidden nail file

A knuckleballer who pitched for 22 years in the big leagues, Niekro *(right)* was caught cheating in dramatic fashion. While pitching for the Minnesota Twins in 1987, the 42-year-old was asked to empty his pockets when the California Angels thought something funny was going on with his pitches. Niekro reached into his pocket and, in one motion, tossed a nail file, as he was trying to show that his hands were empty. The umpire saw the flying nail file, which he was using to doctor the ball, and ejected Niekro, who later received a 10-game suspension.

8 The Bossards' homefield advantage

The Bossard family might be the most valuable groundskeepers of all time. Nothing they did was illegal, but they always gave their team an advantage. Emil Bossard was the Cleveland Indians' groundskeeper from 1932 to '68. When the Yankees visited, he would move the portable fences back, making it difficult for them to hit home runs. His son Gene worked for the White Sox from 1940 to '83. During Gene's tenure, he kept the Comiskey Park infield heavily watered and the grass high. It became known as Bossard's Swamp. He'd also use a humidifier to make balls slightly heavier, causing more ground balls. Gene's son, Roger, has been Chicago's head groundskeeper since 1983. When opposing speedsters came

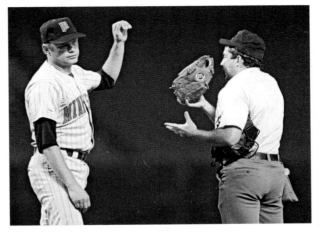

to town, he would water the area around first base to slow them down.

9 Rick Honeycutt's thumb tack

Often when a player gets caught cheating, he'll claim it was a one-time thing. In Honeycutt's case, it's probably true. While pitching a late-season game for the Mariners in 1980, he decided to try to get an edge by taping a thumbtack to one of the fingers in his glove hand, planning to use it to scuff the ball. Somehow, he forgot that he was cheating. Honeycutt went to wipe his forehead and put a gash in his head with the tack. He would later be ejected and suspended for 10 games.

10 George Brett's pine-tar bat

He wasn't a cheater, but Brett had the all-time funniest reaction to being accused of doing so. His Kansas City Royals were visiting the New York Yankees on July 24, 1983, and Brett, a future Hall of Famer, had just belted a go-ahead two-run home run with two outs in the top of the ninth. After Brett rounded the bases, Yankees manager Billy Martin came to home plate for a discussion with rookie umpire Tim McClelland. Martin pointed out that Brett's bat had too much pine tar, which is used to improve a hitter's grip. He argued that the play was illegal and that Brett should be out. But the rule against pine tar wasn't in place because it gave the hitter an advantage — it was because if the ball got pine tar on it, it couldn't be used. Amazingly, the rookie ump sided with Martin, pointed to Brett in the dugout, and gave an out signal, ending the game. Brett went berserk, sprinting out of the dugout waving his arms and screaming. He had to be restrained by an umpire and multiple players *(below)*. The Royals protested, and the American League reversed the call, giving Brett his home run back. The game had to be finished on August 18, with the Royals winning 5–4.

1
Randy Johnson
MLB Career: 1988–2009

To say that the 6'10" Johnson was a dominating presence on the mound is an understatement. In his prime the Big Unit had a fastball that often reached 100 miles per hour. While pitching for the Seattle Mariners, he led the American League in strikeouts for four straight seasons (1992 to '95). Johnson won his first Cy Young Award in 1995 after finishing 18–2 with 294 strikeouts and an AL-best 2.48 ERA. He would go on to win four NL Cy Young Awards — not to mention the 2001 World Series — with the Arizona Diamondbacks. Johnson's 4,875 career strikeouts rank first among lefthanded pitchers and second overall.

2
Warren Spahn
MLB Career: 1942–65

Spahn's pitching strategy — regularly outsmarting hitters and keeping them guessing — is the model for lefthanded pitchers. With that approach he became the winningest southpaw in baseball history, winning at least 20 games in a season 13 times. He was also known for his longevity. In his 21-season career with the Braves, Mets, and Giants, Spahn played in 17 All-Star Games, the most of any pitcher in the 20th century. Even though he won only one Cy Young Award (the honor didn't exist until 1956, in the middle of Spahn's career), he got his own award named after him. Today the Warren Spahn Award is given to the season's best lefthanded pitcher.

3
Lefty Grove
MLB Career: 1925–41

Grove played with the Baltimore Orioles in the International League for five years. He had a 121–38 record before the Philadelphia Athletics paid $100,600 for the southpaw, the highest amount ever paid for a player at the time. Grove proved to be worth the expense. He twice won the pitching Triple Crown, awarded to a hurler who finishes the season with the lowest ERA, the most strikeouts, and the most wins. In 1931, his 31–4 record earned him the AL MVP award.

4
Sandy Koufax
MLB Career: 1955–66

Koufax is considered one of the best pitchers — righthanded or lefthanded — in history. In 1963 he won the NL MVP, the Cy Young Award, and the pitching Triple Crown (1.88 ERA, 306 strikeouts, and 25 wins). In 1965 he struck out a then-record 382 batters. After Koufax won his third Cy Young, second MVP, and third Triple Crown in 1966, he retired at age 30 because of an arthritic condition in his left arm.

LO UTHPAWS

7 Carl Hubbell
MLB Career: 1928–43

According to TIME magazine, Hubbell practiced his pitching when he was a kid by throwing stones at his family's Missouri barn until he could consistently hit the knotholes on the door. Hubbell's unconventional training helped him become the most well-known screwball pitcher in major league history. Playing for the New York Giants, Hubbell was a nine-time All Star who had five 20-win seasons. His best year was in 1933, when he led the league with 23 wins, 10 shutouts, and a 1.66 ERA while winning the NL MVP award and leading the Giants to the World Series title.

8 Tom Glavine
MLB Career: 1987–2008

Glavine ranks fourth among lefthanded pitchers in career wins, which is even more remarkable when you consider that he didn't get off to the greatest start. In his first four seasons with the Atlanta Braves, he had a 33–41 record. He turned it around in a big way in 1991, when he won 20 games and the first of two Cy Young Awards. Four years later, Glavine helped lead the Braves to a World Series title and was named Series MVP. He won his 300th career game in 2007 while pitching for the New York Mets.

5 Steve Carlton
MLB Career: 1965–88

Carlton, who famously refused to speak to the media, let his pitching do the talking. In 1972, Carlton's first year in Philadelphia, he led the NL in wins (27), complete games (30), strikeouts (310), and ERA (1.97) despite his team's 59–97 record. Fast-forward to 1980: Carlton had led the Phillies to four pennants and the franchise's first World Series title. He had also become the first major league pitcher to win four Cy Young Awards. Carlton's career win and strikeout totals rank second among lefties.

9 Eddie Plank
MLB Career: 1901–17

Gettysburg Eddie was known for slowing down the game with his endless rituals between pitches. He took criticism from players, fans, and reporters, but it didn't stop him from winning 326 games — third best among lefthanders. Even though superstar pitchers like Walter Johnson often overshadowed Plank, he won consistently for 17 years and eventually earned a reputation as one of baseball's greats. He finished his career with eight 20-win seasons and three World Series titles with the Philadelphia Athletics. Plank's 69 shutouts and 410 complete games are first all-time for southpaws.

6 Whitey Ford
MLB Career: 1950–67

Ford was the ace on some of the best teams of all time. His Yankees squads reached 11 World Series during his career and won six of them. He became known as the Chairman of the Board because of his ability to handle high-pressure situations, particularly in the postseason. (Ford had an impressive 2.71 ERA in World Series play.) His .690 winning percentage is the best of any lefthanded starting pitcher in major league history. While the 1961 Yankees are known for sluggers Roger Maris and Mickey Mantle, Ford's 25–4 record with 209 strikeouts earned him the AL Cy Young that season.

10 Rube Waddell
MLB Career: 1897–1910

Waddell was known as much for his off-the-field antics as his fastball. In the off-season he fought fires and wrestled alligators. During exhibition games he'd wave the defense off the field and then strike out the side. Luckily Philadelphia manager Connie Mack had a good relationship with the lefty and was able to harness his talent on the mound. Waddell helped the Athletics win two AL pennants, in 1902 and 1905. He led the league in strikeouts six times in his career.

1   **2**   **3**

7

TOP 10 CAPS

1 Boston Red Sox
Beantown's baseball team was originally known as the Boston Americans. They changed their name to the Red Sox in 1908, after the red stockings worn with their uniforms. The team debuted a red B on its dark blue caps in 1933.

2 Los Angeles Angels
Even though the team plays in Anaheim, California, its name — and the halo on its caps — is inspired by nearby Los Angeles, the City of Angels. The team was founded and owned for 36 years by the famous entertainer Gene Autry.

3 Baltimore Orioles
The famous Oriole cartoon bird smiled on the O's from 1966 to '88, a span in which the team won five AL pennants and three World Series. Baltimore switched to a more realistic Oriole in 1989 but brought back the fan favorite in 2012.

4 Washington Nationals
After the Washington Senators moved to Minnesota in 1961, the U.S. capital was without a baseball team until the Montreal Expos became the Nationals in 2005. Even though the team is young, the curly W is a timeless classic.

5 Arizona Diamondbacks
The team's slithery namesake forms the D in the Diamondbacks' logo. The Snakes have proved dangerous on the diamond. Arizona has won the NL West five times since debuting in 1998, and won the World Series in 2001.

4

5

6

8

9

10

6 Oakland Athletics
The A's are one of the American League's original eight franchises, founded in 1901 in Philadelphia. The team settled in Oakland in 1968 and adopted a recognizable green cap featuring an insignia written in Gothic script.

7 New York Mets
The Yankees aren't the only team in town whose logo features an overlapping N and Y. The Mets' insignia is identical to the one used by the New York Giants, who moved to San Francisco after the 1957 season.

8 Chicago White Sox
The combination of the Gothic font and the overlapping letters written diagonally first appeared on Chicago's uniforms in 1951. President Barack Obama is a fan and proudly sports his White Sox hat.

9 Toronto Blue Jays
When Toronto got a team in 1977, it showed national pride by creating a logo with a Canadian maple leaf next to its elegant blue jay. After several logo updates over the years, the Jays went back to their original for the 2012 season.

10 Chicago Cubs
Chicago has proudly displayed the C, which denotes both the team's home city and its nickname, on its uniforms since the team became the Cubs in 1903. The bold red letter didn't appear on caps until 1927.

Top 10
Legendary H

me Runs

1 Hank Aaron's 715th home run
April 8, 1974

Hammerin' Hank's home-run chase to break Babe Ruth's all-time home-run record was not easy. Aaron received lots of media attention, and though he had support from many fans, he also got hate mail from racist people who did not want to see the record broken by an African-American player. The stage was set for Aaron at the Braves' home opener in 1974. After being walked in his first at-bat, Aaron stepped up to the plate in the fourth inning against Dodgers pitcher Al Downing. On his first swing of the night Aaron smacked a high fastball into the Braves' bullpen in left centerfield. Aaron rounded the bases and was greeted at home by teammates who hoisted the beaming slugger on their shoulders. Said Aaron after the momentous occasion: "I feel I can relax now. I feel my teammates can relax. I feel I can have a great season." In fact, Aaron went on to have a 20–home run, All-Star season. He finished his career with 755 dingers.

2 Bill Mazeroski's World Series–winning home run
October 13, 1960

Mazeroski hit the most thrilling home run in postseason history, in Game 7 of the 1960 World Series against the Yankees. With the score tied in the bottom of the ninth, he hit a hanging slider more than 406 feet over the leftfield wall. It is the only Game 7 walk-off home run in World Series history. Still, the eight-time Gold Glove award winner was never a fan of being in the spotlight. "I just played a little part on that team," Maz told the *Pittsburgh Post-Gazette* in 2010. "If I hadn't done it, somebody would have because we were destined to win that year."

3 Joe Carter's World Series–winning home run
October 23, 1993

Long after his historic homer, Carter told reporters that he would have hit the pitch from Phillies closer Mitch Williams foul 99 times out of 100. Luckily for the Blue Jays, the 1-in-100 hit was timely — it occurred during the bottom of the ninth inning in Game 6 of the 1993 World Series. With the Blue Jays trailing 6–5, Carter's long drive to leftfield stayed fair and clinched the Blue Jays' second World Series title in a row. Toronto radio announcer Tom Cheek summed the moment up perfectly when he said on air, "Touch 'em all, Joe. You'll never hit a bigger home run in your life!"

7 Kirk Gibson's World Series pinch-hit home run
October 15, 1988

It was an uphill battle for the Dodgers during the 1988 postseason. They were underdogs against the Mets in the NLCS and against the A's in the World Series. Plus, Gibson, the NL MVP that season, had sprained a ligament in his knee and pulled his hamstring so badly that he used a bat as a cane. Still, Dodgers manager Tommy Lasorda called on the wobbly-legged Gibson to pinch-hit with two outs in the ninth inning of Game 1. Unable to run, Gibson did the only thing he could to guarantee that he'd score: He hit a home run. With Gibson limping around the bases, the Dodgers won the game.

8 Derek Jeter's 3,000th hit
July 9, 2011

Jeter entered the July 2011 game against the Tampa Bay Rays only two hits shy of the rare 3,000-hit mark. A first-inning single placed him one hit away from history, and in the third, he once again faced Tampa ace David Price as the crowd at Yankee Stadium chanted "Der-ek Je-ter." After a long at-bat, Jeter hit a 3–2 breaking ball over the wall in left centerfield to become the first Yankee to reach 3,000 hits and only the second player to achieve the milestone on a home run.

4 Bobby Thomson's Shot Heard 'Round the World
October 3, 1951
In 1951, the Brooklyn Dodgers and the New York Giants faced off in a three-game playoff for the NL pennant. Game 3 aired on national television, and the Dodgers led 4–2 in the bottom of the ninth when the Giants' Thomson came to bat with two runners on base. Thomson smacked a sharp line drive into the leftfield seats. The Shot Heard 'Round the World completed the Giants' magical ride to the World Series.

5 Carlton Fisk's World Series walk-off home run
October 22, 1975
Fisk wasn't expected to return to baseball after suffering a knee injury during a collision at home plate in 1974. Not only did he return, but in 1975 he hit .331 and made the single biggest play of his career. In Game 6 of the World Series against the Reds, Fisk hit a 12th-inning shot that hugged the foul line. As Fisk famously jumped and waved his arms, gesturing the ball to stay fair, the ball hit the leftfield foul pole in Fenway for a thrilling home run.

6 Babe Ruth's called shot
October 1, 1932
Of all of Ruth's home runs, this was the most legendary. Ruth's Yankees were tied 4–4 with the Cubs in the fifth inning of Game 3 in the 1932 World Series at Wrigley Field. With a 2–2 count, Ruth stepped out of the box and lifted his arm toward centerfield, but whether he was calling his shot or merely pointing at Cubs pitcher Charlie Root is still unclear. Either way, Ruth blasted the next pitch he saw an estimated 490 feet over the centerfield wall. It is thought to be one of the longest balls ever hit at Wrigley Field.

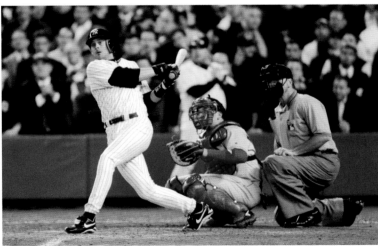

9 Aaron Boone's ALCS walk-off home run
October 16, 2003
The Yankees' Boone did his part to keep the Curse of the Bambino alive in 2003. The ALCS was tied at three games apiece, and the Yankees and Red Sox were tied 5–5 in the bottom of the 11th. That's when Boone stepped up to the plate and launched a ball deep into the leftfield stands. The Yankees won 6–5 to advance to the World Series.

10 Ted Williams's last at-bat
September 28, 1960
Williams was a surefire Hall of Famer when he retired from baseball in 1960, and it's not surprising that he went out on top. In the final plate appearance of his career, he blasted a 1–1 pitch from the Orioles' Jack Fisher into the Red Sox's bullpen — a fitting finish for arguably the greatest hitter who ever lived.

SEP. 2ª 54
KNICK
24-13
B. B. C.

Top 10 History-Making Baseballs

1
The Knickerbocker Ball *(1854)*

Alexander Cartwright, who helped write the game's first set of rules, used this ball with his Knickerbocker Base Ball Club.

2 **1918 World Series**
Pitcher Babe Ruth led the Boston Red Sox to their fifth World Series title, winning Games 1 and 4 against the Chicago Cubs.

3 **Stan Musial's 3,000th hit** *(1958)*
The Cardinals legend is the only player to reach 3,000 hits with a pinch hit. He doubled against the Cubs to spark a St. Louis comeback.

4 **1923 World Series, Game 4**
The box score on this game ball details how the Yankees beat the New York Giants 8–4. Two games later the Yanks won their first title ever.

5 **Hank Aaron's 714th home run** *(1974)*
In his first at-bat of the 1974 season, the Atlanta Braves outfielder hit this ball deep to tie Babe Ruth's record for career home runs.

6 **Regulation ball** *(1858)*
This ball was used the first year that called strikes were introduced as a new part of the game.

7 **"Lemon-peel" cover** *(1855)*
Nicknamed for the way the ball was stitched, this early baseball was made of dark leather so that players could spot it easily against a blue sky.

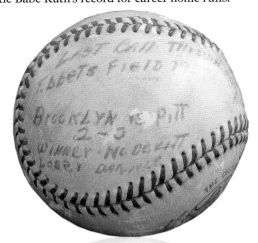

8 **Last ball thrown at Ebbets Field** *(1957)*
The Brooklyn Dodgers' Ebbets Field, where Jackie Robinson made his debut in 1947, shut its doors after the team moved to Los Angeles.

9 **Dead-ball era** *(1916)*
During the low-scoring period of the early 1900s, pitchers ruled. Balls like these were rarely hit out of the ballpark.

10 **Nolan Ryan's seventh no-hitter** *(1991)*
The Ryan Express holds the major league record for most no-hitters (seven). This ball, from his seventh, came 18 years after his first no-no, in 1973.

Top
10 BACKS

TOPS

1 Johnny Bench
MLB Career: 1967–83

Bench played his entire career with the Cincinnati Reds, fueling the Big Red Machine's four National League pennants and two World Series titles. He was unmatched behind the plate — winning 10 consecutive Gold Gloves from 1968 to '77 — and he was just as valuable swinging the bat, leading the NL in batting average three times. Just two years after winning the Rookie of the Year award, Bench earned his first of two MVP awards, in 1970, when he led the league with 45 home runs and 148 RBIs. A 14-time All-Star, including 13 appearances in a row from 1968 to '80, Bench retired in 1983 with the most career home runs by a catcher. In 1989, he was inducted into the Hall of Fame, where his plaque reads, "[Bench] redefined standards by which catchers are measured."

2 Yogi Berra
MLB Career: 1946–65

Berra was no stranger to the biggest stage in baseball: He made 21 World Series appearances as a player, coach, or manager. His 10 championships as a catcher with the New York Yankees are the most ever by a player. Part of being a successful backstop is being durable enough to take a beating behind the plate. The three-time MVP led the American League in games caught for eight seasons. Berra took his share of licks and kept on playing. In 1999, he and Johnny Bench were the two catchers voted by fans to Major League Baseball's All-Century Team.

3 Ivan Rodriguez
MLB Career: 1991–2011

Rodriguez earned a reputation as one of the best catchers of all time thanks to a special combination of quickness and arm strength. Players attempting to steal a base were frequently out of luck against Pudge. In 21 seasons, he caught runners stealing 45.6 percent of the time. Rodriguez won 13 Gold Glove awards (10 of them with the Texas Rangers from 1992 to 2001), was a 14-time All-Star, and was named the American League MVP in 1999 after becoming the first catcher in history with more than 30 home runs, 100 RBIs, and 100 runs scored in a single season. In 2009, he passed Carlton Fisk as baseball's all-time leader in games caught (2,426).

4 Mickey Cochrane
MLB Career: 1925–37

A five-sport athlete at Boston University, Cochrane chose to play professional baseball over football. It's safe to say he made the right decision. With the Philadelphia Athletics, Cochrane was widely recognized as the best catcher in the game. He hit .331 in 1929, .357 in '30, and .349 in '31 — leading his squad to pennants each season. And Cochrane wasn't just calling shots from behind the plate. He became a player-manager when he joined the Detroit Tigers in

1934, and led the team to two straight pennants. Cochrane's playing career came to an end in 1937 when he was hit in the head by a pitch at age 34, but not before he won an MVP award and three World Series titles. After he retired from baseball, Cochrane became a different kind of hero, serving in the U.S. Navy during World War II.

5 Carlton Fisk
MLB Career: 1969–93

A native of New England, Fisk was a hometown hero in Boston. He was the original Pudge before Ivan Rodriguez and became the first-ever unanimous pick for AL Rookie of the Year, in 1972. His hard-nosed style of play earned him a reputation as one of the toughest catchers in the game, but he was also a smart pitch-caller. Fisk is ranked third in career home runs for a catcher (376) and first in seasons behind the plate (24). The most memorable moment of his career took place in 1975, when he hit a 12th-inning walk-off home run against the Reds in Game 6 of the World Series.

7 Josh Gibson
Negro Leagues Career: 1927–46

He didn't play a single inning in the majors, but that didn't stop Gibson from becoming one of the best baseball players ever. Playing in the Negro Leagues, the Puerto Rico League, the Mexican League, and the Dominican League, Gibson faced some great players who at the time were not allowed to participate in major league baseball because of their race. Negro League statistics are hard to determine because of the amount of exhibition games that were played, but it's estimated that Gibson's career batting average was .359 and that he hit a home run every 15.9 at-bats, earning him comparisons to Babe Ruth. In 2000, *The Sporting News* ranked Gibson 18th on its "100 Greatest Baseball Players" list.

8 Roy Campanella
MLB Career: 1948–57

Campanella was one of the majors' first great African-American players. He joined the Brooklyn Dodgers in 1948 — one year after Jackie Robinson broke baseball's color barrier — and by 1949 he had joined Robinson as an All-Star, too. Campanella made his mark on offense and defense. In 1953 he had 142 RBIs, second-most in Dodgers history, and earned his second of three NL MVP awards. Two years later he led the Dodgers to the franchise's first-ever World Series title while winning yet another MVP award. Behind the plate Campanella threw out 51 percent of base runners attempting to steal on him.

9 Gary Carter
MLB Career: 1974–92

Known as The Kid because of his childlike excitement for the game, Carter was a fan favorite while playing for the Montreal Expos and the New York Mets. His attitude paid off: The Hall of Famer played in 11 All-Star Games. Carter also earned three Gold Gloves and was a big part of the Mets team that won the 1986 World Series. After a two-home-run effort in Game 4, Carter started a two-out rally in the tenth inning of Game 6, leading New York to a win and forcing Game 7.

6 Mike Piazza
MLB Career: 1992–2007

As a young first baseman at Miami-Dade College in Florida, Piazza didn't appear to have the stuff of greatness. In fact, the Dodgers took him 1,390th overall in the 1988 draft as a favor to a Piazza family friend, Dodgers manager Tommy Lasorda. But Piazza soon proved to be one of the game's best. In the minors he transformed into a solid catcher with a powerful bat. His 35 home runs in 1993 earned him the NL Rookie of the Year award. His most impressive seasons, though, were in 1996 and '97, when he combined for 76 home runs and 229 RBIs, hitting .336 and .362 respectively. Piazza earned 12 All-Star selections and hit .308 lifetime, but he is best known for his 427 career home runs — tops among catchers in major league history.

10 Joe Mauer
MLB Career: 2004–present

Eight years after making his major league debut, at age 21, Mauer had already made it into the record books. He is the only catcher in major league history to win three batting titles (2006, '08, and '09). In 2009, Mauer became the first catcher in history to lead the league in batting average, on-base percentage, and slugging percentage, so it was no surprise that he won the AL MVP that season. Through 2011, Mauer had earned four All-Star selections and three Gold Gloves.

TOP 10
ANNOUNCERS

1 Vin Scully
The most iconic voice in baseball history, Scully has been calling Dodgers games since 1950, when the team was still in Brooklyn. To this day he works a one-man booth, with no color commentator by his side. Scully has called some of the most famous World Series moments, including Don Larsen's perfect game in 1956, Bill Buckner's error in 1986, and Kirk Gibson's walk-off home run in 1988. Scully not only is smart and understated (he doesn't use catchphrases), but he's also famous for some of the funniest remarks ever made in the broadcast booth, like this one: "The Dodgers are such a .500 team that if there was a way to split a three-game series, they'd find it."

2 Ernie Harwell
The voice of the Detroit Tigers for 42 seasons, Harwell started his big-league broadcasting career in 1948, when the Brooklyn Dodgers traded a minor league catcher for Harwell, who was doing play-by-play for the minor league Atlanta Crackers.

3 Jack Buck
Buck, who has been honored by both the baseball and pro football halls of fame, made some of baseball's most famous calls, including "Go crazy, folks! Go crazy!" after Ozzie Smith's walk-off home run in the 1985 NLCS. Buck's son Joe is a lead announcer for Fox Sports.

4 Mel Allen
The Alabama-born Allen's booming voice as the Yankees' play-by-play man made him a star. He became the host of the national highlight show *This Week in Baseball* in 1977. The show was a big deal at the time because it was the only way to see action from around the majors.

5 Red Barber
Next time you hear ESPN's Chris Berman say, "Back, back, back," remember that it was first said by the Old Redhead. Barber called games for the Brooklyn Dodgers and, later, the Yankees. He was honored by the Baseball Hall of Fame in 1978.

6 Bob Uecker
Uecker's baseball career as a player didn't produce many runs. But as the play-by-play man in Milwaukee since 1971, he has produced many laughs. His sense of humor has made him a Brewers icon and has landed him roles in commercials, on TV, and in movies.

7 Harry Caray
Caray, with his thick glasses and big smile, became famous for calling Cubs games in the 1980s and '90s. He added a unique flavor to games, especially with his catchphrase "Holy cow!" Caray was also known for leading the crowd in "Take Me Out to the Ball Game."

8 Curt Gowdy
Gowdy is best remembered for calling Red Sox games. He didn't bring a lot of flash to the booth, but Gowdy was always pitch-perfect when calling the action. He also announced games for NBC for 10 years, becoming one of the most famous voices in baseball history.

9 Jon Miller
If you watch baseball, you know Miller's deep, booming voice. Miller was the play-by-play man on ESPN's *Sunday Night Baseball* for 21 years and is still the voice of the San Francisco Giants. Easygoing and quick-witted, he's one of the best ever in a one-man broadcast booth.

10 Harry Kalas
To Phillies fans, Kalas was one of them, only he watched games from the booth. He had a deep, gravelly voice (fans outside of Philly would recognize it from NFL Films videos) and would ramp up the excitement when the Phillies were doing well.

Top 10 Innovations

1 Night games
On May 24, 1935, President Franklin Roosevelt flipped the switch for a Reds-Phillies game at Cincinnati's Crosley Field, setting the stage for the first night game in major league history. Between 1935 and '48, every major league ballpark added lights, except for one notable exception. Wrigley Field *(above)*, home of the Chicago Cubs, didn't host its first night game until August 8, 1988.

2 Batting helmet
White Sox second baseman Jackie Hayes is believed to be the first player to wear a batting helmet, in 1940. Hayes needed the protection because of an eye condition. The batting helmet has since become one of the most important pieces of safety equipment in the game.

3 Moneyball
With big-market teams routinely landing star players with huge contracts, Oakland A's general manager Billy Beane figured out a way to compete with the big boys. He used advanced statistics to find players whose value was being overlooked. For instance, Beane knew that a player who drew a lot of walks would be just as valuable as one who hit for a high batting average. That thinking, dubbed Moneyball, helped the underdog A's go to the playoffs four straight seasons, from 2000 to '03.

4 MLB.tv
Not long ago, if you didn't live in the same area as your favorite team, your only chance to see them was the occasional national TV appearance. But now, thanks to MLB.tv, you can catch all 162 games of *every* team, on your computer. With cool interactive features, such as real-time stats and instant highlights, it has changed the baseball-viewing experience.

5 Tommy John surgery
In 1974, Dodgers pitcher Tommy John was having a great season when he tore a ligament in his pitching elbow. Dr. Frank Jobe performed a revolutionary procedure, taking a tendon out of John's leg to replace the injured ligament in his elbow. John made it back to the majors in 1976 and pitched 14 more seasons, making the All-Star team three times. Today, many pitchers have their careers saved by undergoing Tommy John surgery.

6 New catcher's masks
Catchers take a beating behind the plate. The newer helmets, inspired by hockey goalie masks and first worn by Blue Jays catcher Charlie O'Brien in 1996, have given backstops extra protection. They absorb more impact and better deflect nasty foul tips.

7 Coors Field humidor
Trying to get outs in Colorado was a huge challenge when Coors Field first opened in 1995. Because of Denver's high altitude, breaking balls didn't break as much and batted balls traveled farther. From 1995 to 2001, contests at Coors Field averaged a whopping 13.83 runs per game and 3.20 home runs per game compared with 9.70 runs and 2.14 homers in the other 29 stadiums. To control the scoring, the Rockies started storing game balls in a humidor to keep them from getting so dry. Since the introduction of the humidor in 2002, games at Coors Field have averaged 9.4 runs and 1.78 home runs.

8 Pitch f/x
Players, scouts, and fans see pitches in a whole new light thanks to Pitch f/x. Introduced in 2006, the camera system tracks pitches and shows exactly how hard they are thrown and how much balls break.

9 Instant replay
Let's face it: Umpires make mistakes. But there's nothing worse than a missed call deciding a big game. In 2008, MLB adopted instant replay. In the 2009 World Series, it helped correct a blown call on a homer by Yankees slugger Alex Rodriguez (the ball hit a camera above the wall and was originally ruled a double).

10 Bullpen cars
In the 1970s and '80s, relief pitchers entered the game in bullpen cars. Sometimes it was a real automobile (such as the Yankees' pinstriped Datsun); sometimes it was a golf cart shaped like a helmet. The Mariners even rigged up a car to look like a tugboat. Sadly, the last of the bullpen vehicles, the Brewers' Harley-Davidson motorcycle, was retired in 1995.

Top 10 Oddest Deliveries

1 Juan Marichal
MLB Career: 1960–75

When Marichal was in the minor leagues in 1959, his coaches tried to improve his effectiveness against lefthanded hitters by changing his sidearm delivery to a traditional over-the-top throwing motion. In order to maintain control over his pitches, Marichal developed a strange leg kick. As he went into his delivery, Marichal brought his left leg straight up in the air, almost as if he were doing a standing split. Then, in one fluid motion, he would drop his leg, drive it toward the batter, and launch the ball toward home plate. At first, coaches didn't like the windup, but they couldn't argue with the results. The longtime San Francisco Giants pitcher won 243 career games, made nine All-Star teams, and was elected to the Hall of Fame in 1983.

2 Warren Spahn
MLB Career: 1942–65

The Milwaukee Braves hurler is remembered as much for his windup as for his 363 career wins. Spahn started every pitch by bending at the waist and extending both of his arms straight back and above his head. He would then embark on a sweeping, whirlybird motion that brought his arms back in front of him and over his head. The unique delivery helped make him the winningest lefty in baseball history.

3 Orlando Hernandez
MLB Career: 1998–2007

Hernandez looked like he was practicing yoga on the mound. He would practically hide behind his knee, with his leg bent tightly to form a triangle between his left foot, knee, and hip. In only nine seasons, Hernandez won four World Series titles (three with the New York Yankees, one with the Chicago White Sox) and the American League Championship Series MVP award in 1999.

4 Hideki Okajima
MLB Career: 2007–present

Why bother looking at the strike zone? At the end of his otherwise normal windup, Okajima would turn his head to the right and stare directly at the ground as he released the ball. Even with his wacky head positioning, Okajima was effective for the 2007 World Series champion Boston Red Sox, with a 2.22 ERA out of the bullpen.

5 Hideo Nomo
MLB Career: 1995–2008

Nomo's herky-jerky delivery featured so many twists and turns, it's a wonder he never needed a neck brace. Nomo usually started his motion with his arms stretched high above his head, then he'd bring them down while turning his back to the batter and pointing the ball toward the ground before unleashing a pitch. Nomo was named NL Rookie of the Year with the Los Angeles Dodgers in 1995 and threw two no-hitters in 12 big league seasons.

6 Dontrelle Willis
MLB Career: 2003–11

With his flat-brimmed cap pulled low on his head, Willis burst onto the scene with the Florida Marlins in 2003. In order to generate power, the lefty would lift his right leg close enough for his nose to touch his knee. Willis also turned his back to the batter at the peak of his windup, partially obscuring his face with his right shoulder. The deception kept batters off-balance and helped Willis win the 2003 NL Rookie of the Year award.

7 Tim Lincecum
MLB Career: 2007–present

Lincecum weighs only 165 pounds, but he generates remarkable velocity with an abnormally long stride that begins on the pitching rubber and finishes near the infield grass. It all starts when the San Francisco Giants ace lifts his left knee and turns away from home plate. As he uncoils, he straightens out his left leg and sweeps it wide. In Lincecum's first five seasons in the majors, his wild windup landed him two Cy Young Awards and one World Series title.

8 Mark Fidrych
MLB Career: 1976–80

By sticking out his rear end and pointing his left leg straight toward the third-base line, Fidrych made a name for himself with a 1976 rookie year that included 19 wins and a start in the All-Star Game. But Fidrych was also a Detroit Tigers fan favorite for his other strange behaviors on the mound. He was known for getting down on his hands and knees to manicure the dirt and would often talk (yes, talk) to the baseball. Presumably, he was asking for strikes.

9 Bob Gibson
MLB Career: 1959–75

The St. Louis Cardinals pitcher threw inside, and he threw hard. Gibson had a pretty standard throwing motion, but after he released the ball, the power behind his pitches would propel him toward first base. Gibson has some of the most impressive numbers in baseball history. He set a modern-era record for lowest ERA in a season (1.12 in 1968) and won two World Series MVPs, two Cy Young Awards, and one NL MVP.

10 Fernando Valenzuela
MLB Career: 1980–97

In the early 1980s, Fernandomania swept through Los Angeles. Valenzuela had a windup that was amplified by his portly frame (5' 11" and a solid 200 pounds). He would raise both arms up above his head to start his delivery. At the last moment, he'd look up for a split second before uncorking one of his trademark screwballs. In 1981, Valenzuela earned both the NL Rookie of the Year and Cy Young awards while helping the Dodgers win the World Series.

TOP 10 BALLPARKS

1 Fenway Park
Boston Red Sox

Built in 1912, the Red Sox's home has survived three fires (in 1926, 1934, and 2012) to become the oldest active park in the majors. Fenway features recognizable landmarks like the Green Monster (the 37-foot-tall leftfield wall) and a lone red seat in rightfield that marks the longest home run in Fenway history, a 502-foot blast by Ted Williams in 1946.

2 Wrigley Field
Chicago Cubs
Attending a game at Wrigley is like traveling back in time. The outfield walls are made of brick and have been lined with ivy since 1937. Other old-school elements include a manually operated scoreboard and first-come, first-serve bleacher seats.

3 Dodger Stadium
Los Angeles Dodgers
The view at Dodger Stadium stretches from downtown L.A. to the San Gabriel Mountains and is striking enough to distract you from the game. Built in 1962, it is the third oldest ballpark in baseball and the largest in capacity, with 56,000 seats.

4 Camden Yards
Baltimore Orioles
When the Orioles opened their new home in 1992, they set a trend that many teams still follow: Camden combines elements of classic parks from the early 1900s, such as brick facades and steel trusses, with modern touches like an LED scoreboard.

5 AT&T Park
San Francisco Giants
Since 2000, sluggers have been smacking balls over the rightfield wall and into San Francisco Bay. It's the only park in the majors that allows kayakers to go home with a souvenir. Leftfield offers an 80-foot Coca-Cola bottle complete with slides for fans.

6 Kauffman Stadium
Kansas City Royals
A 322-foot-wide fountain overlooking centerfield is the showstopper for this Midwestern masterpiece. In addition to the fountain, fans can also feast their eyes on the sparkling 84-by-104-foot HD scoreboard, installed in 2008.

7 PNC Park
Pittsburgh Pirates
PNC Park features a two-deck design to keep fans close to the action. As a tribute to Hall of Famer Roberto Clemente, who wore number 21, the rightfield wall stands 21 feet tall. The outfield seats offer a spectacular view of the Allegheny River.

8 Miller Park
Milwaukee Brewers
Opened in 2001, the Brewers' home has one of the fastest retractable roofs in baseball. The 10.5-acre covering can open or close in 10 minutes. Miller Park also has a yellow slide above leftfield, where mascot Bernie Brewer celebrates every home-team home run.

9 Comerica Park
Detroit Tigers
Baseball park or amusement park? Comerica features a 50-foot-tall Ferris wheel with cars shaped like baseballs. When the action on the field picks up, expect to celebrate with a water show in the fountain behind centerfield.

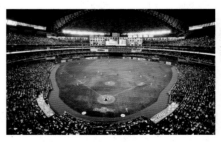

10 Rogers Centre
Toronto Blue Jays
The only active major league park in Canada introduced the baseball world to the retractable roof in 1989. Rogers Centre also has an inside-the-park hotel with rooms that look onto the field through floor-to-ceiling windows.

Top 10 Mas

1 Mr. Met
New York Mets
Mr. Met, the first mascot to appear at games in real life, has been dancing and cheering since 1964. He's carried a big load on his shoulders — and we don't just mean his giant head. It hasn't always been easy to cheer on one of baseball's most hapless teams, but through it all, the eight-fingered phenom has given out more "high fours" than anyone in baseball.

2 Phillie Phanatic
Philadelphia Phillies
Almost all baseball fans know the wacky Phanatic. The big green guy's bright feathers (and occasional dresses) dazzle crowds, and his roly-poly figure dominates opposing mascots. The Phanatic is surprisingly athletic too. While dancing on a dugout roof, he once made a diving catch to snag a foul ball.

3 Bernie Brewer
Milwaukee Brewers
No one celebrates a big hit better than Bernie. After every Brewers home run at Miller Park, Bernie takes a ride down a giant yellow slide. (In the old days he landed in a giant mug, but now he ends up on a platform.) He also has the best facial hair of any mascot. With his big blond mustache, he resembles a yellow-haired Rollie Fingers.

4 Billy the Marlin
Miami Marlins
Billy is a relatively young mascot (the Marlins have only been around since 1993), but he has established some of the most well-known routines in the mascot world, like his water-gun shenanigans with opposing teams. In 2012, when the team changed its colors, he got a makeover as an orange-, yellow-, and blue-striped fish.

5 Wally the Green Monster
Boston Red Sox
A die-hard Sox fan who lives inside Fenway Park's Green Monster outfield wall, Wally made his debut in 1997. The 37-foot-tall leftfield wall he's named after is famous for "eating up" would-be home runs. Judging from his enormous waistline, Wally has also gobbled up more than his share of Fenway Franks.

cots

6 **Mariner Moose**
Seattle Mariners
Mariner Moose is on the loose! During the 1990s, one of his favorite pastimes was strapping on in-line skates and getting towed by an all-terrain vehicle across the outfield at Seattle's Kingdome. But being a daredevil has its dangers: During the 1995 playoffs, the Moose broke his ankle when he crashed full speed into the centerfield wall.

7 **The San Diego Chicken**
San Diego Padres
The Chicken is one of the most famous sports mascots of all time. He is so popular in San Diego that he once made more than 500 consecutive appearances at Padres games. One of his best moves was stealing baseballs during opponents' warmups, eating them, and giving them back . . . by lifting his tail.

8 **Stomper**
Oakland A's
Stomper has long battled with his cross-bay rival, the San Francisco Giants' Lou Seal, for mascot supremacy in Northern California. You have to admit that the big baby elephant (whose weight is listed as "a ton of fun") definitely has the edge in adorableness, with his big eyes and miniature trunk.

9 **Lou Seal**
San Francisco Giants
There's no questioning Lou Seal's sense of style. He dons a backward cap, designer sunglasses, and carefully combed whiskers. He's got some smooth moves too, such as his fan-pleasing belly tosses. But make no mistake, Lou is not just a pretty boy. He can roughhouse with the best of them, dishing out thousands of noogies since his debut in 1996.

10 **The Oriole Bird**
Baltimore Orioles
Hatched from an egg at Baltimore's Memorial Stadium in 1979, the Oriole Bird was born to dance. No mascot can match his moves on the dugout roof, particularly his patented tail-feather shake. He gets all that energy from a strict diet of birdseed, crab cakes, and the occasional nibble of a fan's head.

Top 10 Sluggers

1 Hank Aaron
Rightfielder
MLB Career: 1954–76

Hammerin' Hank's consistent power at the plate made him the greatest slugger in major league history. Aaron's baseball career began when he was a 17-year-old playing for the Indianapolis Clowns of the Negro Leagues. After leading the team to the 1952 championship, he was recruited by major league scouts and landed in the Milwaukee Braves' farm system later that year. It didn't take long for Aaron to establish himself as one of the most dangerous bats in the majors. From 1955 to '74, he never hit fewer than 20 home runs in a season, helping him become the second-youngest player to hit 500 career home runs. "Trying to throw a fastball by Henry Aaron is like trying to sneak a sunrise past a rooster," St. Louis pitcher Curt Simmons once said. The highlight of Aaron's career came on April 8, 1974, when he broke Babe Ruth's career home run record with his 715th longball. Aaron retired with 755 home runs and was elected into the Hall of Fame in 1982.

2 Babe Ruth
Pitcher/Outfielder
MLB Career: 1914–35

The original home-run king, the portly Ruth is one of the most famous athletes of all time. His 1921 season still ranks among the best ever. The Yankees legend beat his own single-season record with 59 homers and finished with 171 RBIs and a .378 batting average. His 714 career home runs are third-best in history.

3 Willie Mays
Centerfielder
MLB Career: 1951–73

One of the most complete players of all time, Mays was a 24-time All-Star who ended his career with 660 home runs, fourth-most in history. As a member of the Giants, he led the National League in homers four times and in slugging percentage five times. Mays ranks in the top 10 in career runs, home runs, and RBIs.

4 Mickey Mantle
Centerfielder
MLB Career: 1951–68

The term "tape-measure home run" was coined in 1953 after Mantle blasted a 565-foot shot. In 1961 he and Yankees teammate Roger Maris chased Babe Ruth's single-season home-run record. An injured Mantle finished five short of Ruth, but he still helped lead New York to the World Series title.

5 Ken Griffey Jr.
Centerfielder
MLB Career:
1989–2010

Griffey was a three-time Home Run Derby champion and hit 56 home runs in back-to-back seasons (1997 and '98). Griffey won the American League MVP award in 1997 with the Mariners and ranks fifth on the all-time home-run list with 630 longballs.

6 Ted Williams
Leftfielder
MLB Career: 1939–42,
'46–60

Williams had the perfect combination of power, consistency, and patience. In his 19 years with the Red Sox, he hit 521 home runs and 525 doubles. His .634 career slugging percentage is second to Babe Ruth. Williams won two Triple Crowns and two MVP awards during his career.

7 Josh Gibson
Catcher
Negro Leagues Career: 1930–46

Though his official statistics are unverified, the Hall of Fame estimates that Gibson hit about 800 homers with a .359 career batting average in a 17-year career. He led the National Negro League in home runs for 10 consecutive years. He is credited with 75 home runs in 1931, and in 1937 *The Sporting News* wrote about Gibson belting a 580-foot home-run shot at Yankee Stadium.

8 Jim Thome
First Baseman
MLB Career: 1991–present

When he comes to the plate, Thome points his bat toward rightfield while the pitcher gets his sign. He might as well be calling his shot, because balls off Thome's bat usually end up in the rightfield stands. Thome has had 12 seasons with 30 or more home runs. He has the record for the longest home runs hit at Progressive Field in Cleveland (511 feet) and Target Field in Minneapolis (490 feet).

9 Frank Robinson
Outfielder
MLB Career: 1956–76

Robinson was an aggressive hitter who would crowd the plate to make sure he got pitches he liked. The strategy was risky — he led the league in hit by pitches seven times — but it worked. Robinson hit 30 or more home runs in 11 seasons, including 49 (along with a league-leading 122 RBIs) in 1966. As a member of the Orioles that year, he hit a ball completely out of Baltimore's Memorial Stadium, the only player ever to do so.

10 Albert Pujols
First Baseman
MLB Career: 2001–present

Pujols fueled the Cardinals' offense for 11 years before signing with the Angels for the 2012 season. A nine-time All-Star with three MVP awards and two World Series titles, Pujols is the first player in history to hit 30 or more home runs in a season in each of his first 11 seasons. Through 2011, he ranked first among active players in career batting average and slugging percentage.

1927 New York Yankees

POSITION	PLAYER
CF	Earle Combs
SS	Mark Koenig
RF	Babe Ruth
1B	Lou Gehrig
LF	Bob Meusel
2B	Tony Lazzeri
3B	Joe Dugan
C	Pat Collins
P	Waite Hoyt
MANAGER	Miller Huggins

NOTES Babe Ruth broke his own single-season home run record when he swatted his 60th long ball on September 30.

1929 PHILADELPHIA ATHLETICS Ⓐ

POSITION	PLAYER
2B	Max Bishop
CF	Mule Haas
C	Mickey Cochrane
LF	Al Simmons
3B	Sammy Hale
1B	Jimmie Foxx
RF	Bing Miller
SS	Jimmy Dykes
P	Lefty Grove
MANAGER	Connie Mack

NOTES This team had six future Hall of Famers: Grove, Cochrane, Simmons, Foxx, Eddie Collins, and manager Connie Mack.

REDS 1975 Cincinnati Reds ③

POSITION	PLAYER
3B	PETE ROSE
RF	KEN GRIFFEY
2B	JOE MORGAN
C	JOHNNY BENCH
1B	TONY PEREZ
LF	GEORGE FOSTER
SS	DAVEY CONCEPCION
CF	CESAR GERONIMO
P	DON GULLETT
MANAGER	SPARKY ANDERSON

NOTES This was the first of back-to-back World Series wins for the Big Red Machine. The team scored a league-high 840 runs.

TOP 10 LINEUPS

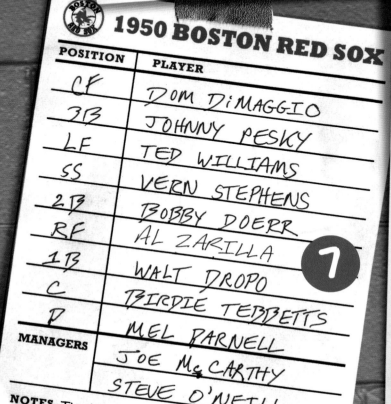

1950 BOSTON RED SOX

POSITION	PLAYER
CF	DOM DiMAGGIO
3B	JOHNNY PESKY
LF	TED WILLIAMS
SS	VERN STEPHENS
2B	BOBBY DOERR
RF	AL ZARILLA
1B	WALT DROPO
C	BIRDIE TEBBETTS
P	MEL PARNELL
MANAGERS	JOE McCARTHY
	STEVE O'NEILL

NOTES The team batting average was .302. Dropo (.322 average) won AL Rookie of the Year.

1998 New York Yankees

POSITION	PLAYER
2B	CHUCK KNOBLAUCH
SS	DEREK JETER
RF	PAUL O'NEILL
1B	TINO MARTINEZ
CF	BERNIE WILLIAMS
DH	DARRYL STRAWBERRY
LF	CHAD CURTIS
C	JORGE POSADA
3B	SCOTT BROSIUS
P	DAVID WELLS
MANAGER	JOE TORRE

4

NOTES: Wells pitched a perfect game against the Twins on May 17, 1998.

1996 SEATTLE MARINERS

5

POSITION	PLAYER
2B	JOEY CORA
SS	ALEX RODRIGUEZ
CF	KEN GRIFFEY JR.
DH	EDGAR MARTINEZ
RF	JAY BUHNER
1B	PAUL SORRENTO
LF	MARK WHITEN
3B	DAVE HOLLINS
C	DAN WILSON
P	STERLING HITCHCOCK
MANAGER	LOU PINIELLA

NOTES: The 1996 AL All-Star team included five players from this lineup: Rodriguez, Griffey, Martinez, Buhner, and Wilson.

1961 New York Yankees

POSITION	PLAYER
2B	BOBBY RICHARDSON
SS	TONY KUBEK
RF	ROGER MARIS
CF	MICKEY MANTLE
LF	YOGI BERRA
1B	BILL SKOWRON
C	ELSTON HOWARD
3B	CLETE BOYER
P	WHITEY FORD
MANAGER	RALPH HOUK

6

NOTES: Maris broke Babe Ruth's home run record, hitting his 61st on October 1, 1961. Mantle finished the season with 54 homers.

BALTIMORE ORIOLES

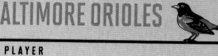

PLAYER
Don Buford
Mark Belanger
Frank Robinson
Boog Powell
Paul Blair
Brooks Robinson
Davey Johnson
Ellie Hendricks
Jim Palmer
Earl Weaver

8

...ooks Robinson (1964), Frank Robinson ...6), and Powell ('70) all won the AL MVP ...ard for Baltimore in a seven-year span.

1955 Brooklyn Dodgers

POSITION	PLAYER
2B	JIM GILLIAM
SS	PEE WEE REESE
CF	DUKE SNIDER
C	ROY CAMPANELLA
RF	CARL FURILLO
1B	GIL HODGES
3B	JACKIE ROBINSON
LF	SANDY AMOROS
P	DON NEWCOMBE
MANAGER	WALTER ALSTON

9

NOTES: Campanella was named the 1955 NL MVP. He, Reese, Robinson, and Snider are all Hall of Famers.

1907 CHICAGO CUBS

POSITION	PLAYER
CF	Jimmy Slagle
LF	Jimmy Sheckard
1B	Frank Chance
3B	Harry Steinfeldt
C	Johnny Kling
2B	Johnny Evers
RF	Frank Schulte
SS	Joe Tinker
P	Orval Overall
MANAGER	Frank Chance

10

NOTES: Chance, a player-manager, led the team to its first World Series win.

Top 10 Ugly U

1 **Chicago White Sox**
Bermuda shorts may have helped the White Sox stay cool in 1976, but they certainly didn't *look* cool. Chicago players wore shorts and collared shirts for only three games. "They were ugly," pitcher Goose Gossage told the *Sacramento Bee* in 1993. "And I'll tell you, we played exactly like we looked."

2 **San Diego Padres**
Today the Padres wear a camouflage jersey as part of their alternate uniform. But in the 1970s the team had no trouble blending in with the infield dirt thanks to their unfortunate color combination of brown and yellow. San Diego changed its colors to more attractive tones of blue and white in 1991.

3 **Kansas City A's**
After purchasing the A's in 1963, owner Charles Finley wanted to leave his mark on the team. He changed its colors from red, white, and blue to Kelly green, wedding-gown white, and Fort Knox gold. He also mixed up the look with sleeveless jerseys worn over bright-colored undershirts.

4 **Baltimore Orioles**
The Orioles wore eye-popping uniforms in 1971, when they won 101 games. But don't expect those to make a comeback. "Someone said it looked like Halloween candy corn," manager Buck Showalter said after his squad put them on for throwback night in 2010. "Take a picture. You won't see them again."

5 **Pittsburgh Pirates**
In 1977, the Pirates had baseball buzzing when they traded in their white-and-gray uniforms for bumblebee colors of gold and black. They also wore pillbox caps, which they would later adorn with Stargell Stars (given out by Pirates great Willie Stargell to players who had a good game).

niforms

6 **Philadelphia Phillies**
The 1979 Phillies called their all-maroon uniforms the Saturday Night Special (the team planned on wearing them on Saturday games). Fans and reporters, however, called them pajamas. They were so widely criticized that the Phillies retired the look after one game.

7 **Tampa Bay Devil Rays**
Before they became the Rays, they were the Devil Rays, with the most colorful logo in baseball. In 1998, a broad spectrum of colors streaked across their uniforms. But the rainbow did not prove to be a good-luck charm — the team didn't have a winning season until 2008.

8 **Florida Marlins**
The Marlins made a splash in 1993, the team's first season, but not because of their play (they lost 98 games that year). They were hard to miss in their loud teal uniforms. In 2012, the new-look Miami Marlins kept the theme of bright colors, adopting orange, yellow, and blue.

9 **Houston Astros**
The Astros wore red-, orange-, and yellow-striped masterpieces in the mid- to late '70s. The stripes represented the fiery trails of a shooting star or a rocket. The look was certainly unique. In fact, the Astros liked standing out so much that they wore the uniforms at home *and* on the road.

10 **Cleveland Indians**
In the mid-'70s, the Indians had opponents seeing red — literally. The team looked like baseball-playing tomatoes in their all-red getups. The team also adopted a strangely angular C on their hats. The Indians got rid of the uniform and the insignia after the 1977 season.

1 Mariano Rivera

MLB Career: 1995–present

For hitters, there's no scarier sight on the mound than the New York Yankees' Mariano Rivera. Baseball's all-time saves leader was the setup man for Yankees closer John Wetteland on the 1996 World Series championship team. His 2.09 ERA during the regular season helped him move into the closer role in 1997. Rivera did not disappoint, keeping his ERA under 2.00 in each of his first three seasons as the closer. His signature pitch, the cut fastball, baffles hitters. The 12-time All-Star has an 89.3 career save percentage (tops among pitchers with a minimum of 200 saves). Rivera has been even better in the postseason. Behind his 0.70 playoff ERA, the Yankees have won five World Series titles with Mo on the mound.

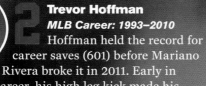

2 Trevor Hoffman

MLB Career: 1993–2010

Hoffman held the record for career saves (601) before Mariano Rivera broke it in 2011. Early in Hoffman's career, his high leg kick made his mid-90s fastball tough to pick up. When shoulder injuries slowed his heater down, he relied on his change-up to shut down batters. Over an 18-year career spent mostly with the Padres, Hoffman had nine 40-save seasons, a record.

3 Dennis Eckersley

MLB Career: 1975–98

Before going to the bullpen, Eckersley was an All-Star starter for the Indians and Red Sox. He even threw a no-hitter in 1977. He was just as dominant after taking over as the A's closer in 1987. The following season, Eckersley led the American League with 45 saves. He went on to win the 1992 AL Cy Young and MVP awards. During his last 10 years in the majors, he walked only 86 batters in more than 600 innings pitched.

4 Billy Wagner

MLB Career: 1995–2010

Wagner was a natural righthanded ballplayer, but after breaking his right arm twice as a kid, he practiced throwing baseballs lefthanded. Fast-forward to 2010, when Billy the Kid retired as the best — and hardest-throwing — lefthanded closer in history. In 2003, Wagner had 44 saves and a 1.78 ERA with the Astros. The fireballer also threw 159 pitches at 100 miles per hour or above that season, tops in the majors.

5 Rollie Fingers

MLB Career: 1968–85

With Fingers closing games, Oakland three-peated as World Series champions from 1972 to '74. Fingers was the MVP of that '74 Series after saving two games and winning one. Seven seasons later in Milwaukee, Fingers won the AL MVP and Cy Young awards, finishing the season with 28 saves and a 1.04 ERA.

6 Bruce Sutter

MLB Career: 1976–88

Sutter used a split-fingered fastball to shut down hitters late in games. He once struck out six batters in a row — including three on nine straight pitches. Sutter is the only player to have led the National League in saves five times (twice with the Cubs and in three seasons with the Cardinals). He was also the first pitcher elected to the Hall of Fame without ever having started a game.

7 Goose Gossage

MLB Career: 1972–94

Gossage, best known for his years with the Yankees from 1978 to '83, holds the club record for ERA (2.14) and hits per nine innings (6.59). He led the AL in saves three times. While those numbers don't sound dominant by today's standards, Gossage often pitched three innings to close out a game (as opposed to the one inning most closers throw today). He also made nine All-Star teams in the first 14 seasons of his career.

8 Lee Smith

MLB Career: 1980–97

As a member of the Cubs, Red Sox, and Cardinals, the 6'6" Smith struck out more than one batter per inning from 1985 to '90, and saved at least 40 games each season from 1991 to '93.

9 Dan Quisenberry

MLB Career: 1979–90

While many closers bring the heat, Quisenberry's greatest weapon was his accuracy. Throwing submarine-style, he walked only 1.4 batters per nine innings in his career. Quisenberry played his best years with the Royals from 1979 to '88, leading the AL in saves five times.

10 Hoyt Wilhelm

MLB Career: 1952–72

Wilhelm was the first pitcher to use the knuckleball as a primary pitch. Playing for nine teams in his 21-year career, he was the first relief pitcher elected to the Hall of Fame. Wilhelm holds the modern-era record for lowest ERA by a relief pitcher (2.52) with at least 1,500 innings pitched.

TOP 10
CLOSERS

Photo Credits

Cover: Bill Frakes
Back Cover: John Iacono (Oddest Deliveries, Mascots); Chuck Solomon (Rivalries); Ronald C. Modra (Families); Ronald C. Modra (Ugly Uniforms); Transcendental Graphics (Sluggers)
Title Page: Walter Iooss Jr.
Copyright Page: Robert Beck
Table of Contents: Al Tielemans
Leadoff Hitters: Walter Iooss Jr. (Henderson, Brock); William R. Smith (Raines); Sheedy & Long (Rose); Transcendental Graphics (Hamilton); Robert Beck (Ichiro); Damian Strohmeyer (Damon); Brad Mangin (Biggio); Bob Rosato (Reyes); Richard Mackson (Molitor)
Unbreakable Records: Walter Iooss Jr. (Ripken); Bettmann/Corbis (DiMaggio); Andy Hayt (Hershiser)
Hit Robbers: Damian Strohmeyer (Jones); Getty Images (Speaker); Corbis/Bettman (Ashburn, Cobb); Herb Scharfman/Getty Images (Flood); Tony Triolo (Mays); Al Tielemans (Edmonds); Rogers Photo Archive/Getty Images (Carey); TSN/Icon SMI (DiMaggio); Al Messerschmidt (Blair)
Little Guys: Hy Peskin (Gaedel); Keystone Press (Keeler); Manny Millan (Patek); Bettmann/Corbis (Rizzuto); Al Tielemans (Eckstein); Neil Leifer (Morgan); Getty Images (Berra); Ronald C. Modra (Puckett); Damian Strohmeyer (Pedroia); Peter Read Miller (Lincecum)
Nicknames: Time Inc. Picture Collection (Ruth); Jerry Wachter (Smith); Bettmann/Corbis (Mays); Peter Read Miller (Griffey); Ron Vesely/Getty Images (Williams); Charles M. Conlon/TSN/Icon SMI (Jackson); Walter Iooss Jr. (Ortiz); Heinz Kluetmeier (Lee); Lane Stewart (Fidrych); Tim DeFrisco (Sandoval)
Hardest Throwers: Ronald C. Modra (Ryan); AP (Paige); John W. McDonough (Chapman); AP (Feller); National Baseball Hall of Fame Library, Cooperstown, NY (Williams, Wood); Chuck Solomon (Zumaya); Richard Mackson (Richard); Art Rickerby (Score)
Rivalries: Chuck Solomon (Yankees–Red Sox); Annmarie Avila (Pennants)
Single-Game Performances: National Baseball Hall of Fame Library, Cooperstown, NY
Toughest Pitches: Walter Iooss Jr.
World Series Moments: Neil Leifer (Mazeroski, Jackson); William R. Smith (Carter); National Baseball Hall of Fame Library, Cooperstown, NY (Larsen); Focus On Sport/Getty Images (Koufax); John Iacono (Buckner, Puckett, Gibson); David E. Klutho (Freese); Frank Hurley/New York Daily News (Mays)
Most Intimidating: Walter Iooss Jr. (Gibson); Bettmann/Corbis (Cobb); Hy Peskin (McCovey); John Iacono (Radatz); Bettmann/Corbis (Stargell); Art Shay (Hrabosky); Al Tielemans (Thomas); Diamond Images/Getty Images (Duren); V.J. Lovero (Johnson); Herb Scharfman (Howard)
Managers: Sporting News/Getty Images (McGraw); Neil Leifer (Stengel); Bettmann/Corbis (Mack); Charles Victor/AP (McCarthy); Al Tielemans (LaRussa); John Iacono (Torre); John Dominis/Time Life Pictures/Getty Images (Alston); Heinz Kluetmeier (Anderson);

Ronald C. Modra (Cox); Manny Millan (Weaver)
Double Play Combos: Lane Stewart (Whitaker and Trammell); Richard Meek (Fox and Aparicio); Bruce Bennett/Getty Images (Herr); AP (Smith, Mazeroski, Alomar, Vizquel); John W. McDonough (Utley and Rollins); Bettmann/Corbis (Groat); Heinz Kluetmeier (Lopes and Russell); Herb Scharfman (Green and Campaneris); Focus on Sport/Getty Images (Morgan); Rich Pilling (Concepcion); Porter Binks (Cano and Jeter)
Families: Ronald C. Modra (Griffeys, Ripkens); Elsa/Getty Images (Prince Fielder); Anthony Neste (Cecil Fielder); Manny Millan (Alomars); Neil Leifer (Alous); Louis Requena/MLB Photos/Getty Images (Niekros, 2); Bettmann/Corbis (DiMaggios); Focus on Sport/Getty Images (Martinez brothers); Charles M. Conlon/TSN/Icon SMI (Waners, 2); Elsa/Getty Images (B.J. Upton); Rob Tringali/Getty Images (Justin Upton)
Minor League Team Names: Courtesy of the Richmond Flying Squirrels; Courtesy of the Montgomery Biscuits; Courtesy of the Jamestown Jammers; Courtesy of the Lehigh Valley Iron Pigs; Courtesy of the Fort Wayne TinCaps; Courtesy of the Toledo Mud Hens; Courtesy of the Omaha Storm Chasers; Courtesy of the Albuquerque Isotopes; Courtesy of the Asheville Tourists; Courtesy of the Savannah Sand Gnats
Switch-Hitters: Neil Leifer (2)
Baseball Movies: ©Universal Pictures/Everett Collection (*Field of Dreams*); ©Buena Vista Pictures/Everett Collection (*Angels in the Outfield*); ©Columbia Pictures/Everett Collection (*A League of Their Own, Moneyball*); ©TriStar Pictures/Everett Collection (*The Natural*); Courtesy of Fox (*Rookie of the Year*); Everett Collection (*The Pride of the Yankees, The Sandlot*); ©Orion Pictures/Everett Collection (*Eight Men Out*) ©Touchstone/Everett Collection (*Mr. 3000*)
Speedsters: V.J. Lovero (Henderson); Walter Iooss Jr. (Brock); National Baseball Hall of Fame Library/MLB Photos/Getty Images (Bell); John G. Zimmerman (Robinson); Heinz Kluetmeier (Wilson); Ben Van Hook (Coleman); Al Tielemans (Sanders); Neil Leifer (Wills); Tim DeFrisco (Crawford); Chuck Solomon (Roberts)
Yogi-isms: Tony Triolo; Walter Iooss Jr.; Charles W. Luzier/Reuters; Hulton Archive/Getty Images
Facial Hair: Robert Beck (Damon); Focus on Sport/Getty Images (Fingers); Ezra Shaw/Getty Images (Wilson); John Biever (Spiezio); St. Louis Cardinals, LLC/Getty Images (Hrabosky); Damian Strohmeyer (Ortiz); Scott Boehm/Getty Images (Axford); Ron Vesely/MLB Photos/Getty Images (Jenks); Scott Rovak/AFP/Getty Images (Hermanson); Rich Pilling/MLB Photos/Getty Images (Murray)
Future Hall of Famers: John Biever (Pujols, Thome); Chuck Solomon (Jeter, Sabathia, Rodriguez, Jones); Damian Strohmeyer (Ichiro, Guererro); John Iacono (Rivera); Al Tielemans (Halladay)
Scandals: Bettmann/Corbis (White Sox); Mark Morency/AP (Belle); Lennox Mclendon/AP (Niekro); Robert F. Rodriguez/Rockland Journal News/AP (Brett)
Southpaws: Heinz Kluetmeier (Johnson); Herb Scharfman (Spahn, Ford); International News Photo (Grove); Neil Leifer (Koufax); Tony Triolo (Carlton); AP (Hubbell);

Bob Rosato (Glavine); National Baseball Hall of Fame Library, Cooperstown, NY (Plank); Mark Rucker/Transcendental Graphics/Getty Images (Waddell)
Caps: Chad Matthew Carlson (10)
Legendary Home Runs: Tony Triolo (Aaron); AP (Mazeroski); John Iacono (Carter, Jeter); Bettmann/Corbis (Thomson); Harry Cabluck/AP (Fisk); B. Bennett/Getty Images (Ruth); Ronald C. Modra (Gibson); Chuck Solomon (Boone); AP (Williams)
History-Making Baseballs: Milo Stewart/National Baseball Hall of Fame Library, Cooperstown, NY (Knickerbocker, Ebbets Field); David N. Berkwitz (1918 World Series, Dead-ball era); National Baseball Hall of Fame Library, Cooperstown, NY (Musial, Aaron, Ryan); Bret Wills (3)
Backstops: Neil Leifer (Bench); AP (Berra, Gibson, Campanella); Brad Mangin (Rodriguez); ACME (Cochrane); Heinz Kluetmeier (Fisk); Chuck Solomon (Piazza); Ronald C. Modra/Sports Imagery/Getty Images (Carter); John Biever (Mauer)
Announcers: Phil Bath (Scully); Detroit News (Harwell); David E. Klutho (Buck); Photofest (Allen); AP (Barber); Morry Gash/AP (Uecker); Charles Bennett/AP (Caray); AP (Gowdy); Scott Clarke/ESPN (Miller); Ron Frehm/AP (Kalas)
Innovations: Ronald C. Modra
Oddest Deliveries: John Iacono (Marichal, Hernandez, Fidrych); Marvin E. Newman (Spahn, Gibson); Bob Rosato (Okajima); Peter Read Miller (Nomo, Valenzuela); Heinz Kluetmeier (Willis); Chuck Solomon (Lincecum)
Ballparks: Winslow Townson (Fenway Park); Chuck Solomon (Wrigley Field); Danny Moloshok/Icon SMI (Dodger Stadium); Hunter Martin/WireImage.com (Camden Yards); Brad Mangin (AT&T Park); G. Newman Lowrance/Getty Images (Kauffman Stadium); Fred Vuich (PNC Park); John Biever (Miller Park); Al Tielemans (Comerica Park); Fred Thornhill/Reuters (Rogers Centre)
Mascots: Erick W. Rasco (Mr. Met); John Iacono (Phillie Phanatic); Scott Boehm/Getty Images (Bernie Brewer); Joel Auerbach/Getty Images (Billy the Marlin); Joe Robbins/Getty Images (Wally the Green Monster); Paul Jasienski/Getty Images (Mariner Moose); Lenny Ignelzi/AP (The San Diego Chicken); Jason O. Watson/US Presswire (Stomper); Robert Beck (Lou Seal); G. Fiume/Getty Images (The Oriole Bird)
Sluggers: Neil Leifer (Aaron); Transcendental Graphics (Ruth); Walter Iooss Jr. (Mays); John G. Zimmerman (Mantle, Williams); John Biever (Griffey, Thome); National Baseball Hall of Fame

Nicknamed The Kid, slugger Ken Griffey Jr. had a youthful enthusiasm for the game.

Library, Cooperstown, NY (Gibson); Getty Images (Robinson); Jeff Gross/Getty Images (Pujols)
Ugly Uniforms: Diamond Images/Getty Images (White Sox); George Gojkovich/Getty Images (Padres); Rogers Photo Archive/Getty Images (A's); John Iacono (Orioles); Ronald C. Modra (Pirates); Heinz Kluetmeier (Phillies); Craig Melvin/Getty Images (Devil Rays); Mitchell Layton/Getty Images (Marlins); Rich Pilling/MLB Photos/Getty Images (Astros); Tony Tomsic/MLB Photos/Getty Images (Indians)
Closers: Chuck Solomon (Rivera, Wagner, Smith, Quisenberry); John W. McDonough (Hoffman); Ron Vesely/MLB Photos/Getty Images (Eckersley); Fred Kaplan (Fingers); Ronald C. Modra (Sutter); Rich Pilling/MLB Photos/Getty Images (Gossage); Rogers Photo Archive/Getty Images (Wilhelm)
Credits Page: Peter Read Miller (Griffey); Heinz Kluetmeier (Rodgers); Al Tielemans (Votto); James Porto (Votto cover illustration)